Victory Through His Divine Romance

Endorsement

Sometimes the body of Christ seems to forget the importance of testimonies for the benefit of all believers. We need to be constantly learning from each other so that all of us can be overcomers (Revelation 12:11). Deborah Hust's book *Victory Through His Divine Romance* is one woman's story of how she triumphed over the enemy in her own life, despite having to deal with many painful experiences. I know her testimony will be a great help to you.

Joan Hunter, author
Evangelist/Host of Miracles Happen TV Show

Victory Through His Divine Romance

by Deborah M. Hust

First Edition
Copyright © 2022 Deborah M. Hust.
Second Printing, August 2022

Paperback ISBN: 979-8-43986-463-8
E-book ISBN: 978-1-64669-236-1

All Scripture references are from the New King James Version (NKJV) of the Bible unless otherwise noted.

www.VictoryThroughHisDivineRomance.org

Table of Contents

Dedication

To my precious and mighty Lord and Savior Jesus Christ, for without You, nothing in this life is possible. I thank You for Your mercy, grace, and everlasting love in my life. I cannot wait to see Your beautiful face at the gates of heaven.

Jehovah Shalom: "The Lord Our Peace"

> *They that wait upon the Lord shall find new strength. They will mount on wings like eagles. They will run and not grow weary; they will walk and not faint.*
>
> *—Isaiah 40:31, NKJV*

Foreword

Sitting across the table at the Starbucks in Cherry Hills Village, Colorado, I could not believe what she was saying. Trying to keep my face from reacting, but in truth, I was fighting back tears as I heard her story for the first time.

That was where I began a journey with Deb Hust. We bonded over connections with the U.S. Marines, Denver First Church, and our love for the Lord. Our first steps together were candid and raw, but somehow filled with hope that only comes from knowing the Lord.

Two years later down this bumpy road, as Deb, some other friends, and I sat together in a courtroom in Arapahoe County, Colorado, God amazed me at what He had transformed in her. Deb had been transformed by suffering that had been surrendered to God, and it changed who she was at her core. What surprised me is what God had transformed in me too.

Only God can take the dark or difficult aspects of each of our lives and turn them into something beautiful and good. Our stories can comfort others, grow us up in faithfulness and be a glory to our Lord.

May you be transformed as you read this powerful story,

Cindy Johnson
Pastor of Christian Education
Denver First Church of the Nazarene
June 2021

Acknowledgements and Thanks

First, my beloved covenant husband and partner: Your unexpected appearance in my life has been nothing short of beautiful. The compassion, silent support, soul peace, and true and honest love you have given has been far more than I could have ever imagined; thank you for putting up with my stubbornness and loving me through everything. I love you from the depths of my soul—you are my blessing, my *Boaz!* You and our family are gifts beyond anything I could have ever dreamed of.

My Bug: You are an amazingly unexpected gift to your mama. I cannot wait to see the plans God has for you unfold before my eyes. You are smart, funny, handsome, beautiful, and set apart for something great. Always remember: Jesus and Mama love you best.

Next, my best friend in this entire world, Robyn: Girl, we have been through some stuff. Thank you for listening when God told you to stand silent and firm by my side to be my way out and my safety net to fall into. Without you, I could not have done half the things I've done. If I had to pick one on this earth, you would be my hero. I love you!

My best friend, Christopher: Thank you for the support, encouragement, and love in some of the darkest parts of this journey. You demonstrate always what Christ's love looks like. You have been a solid shoulder, prayer warrior and an amazing example of leadership and faith. Your own walk to victory is an inspiration and a blessing to all who hear it. I love you more than words could ever describe.

My grandmothers, Janet and Mabel: I have been blessed beyond measure by knowing the both of you and I thank you for all the subtle faith teachings throughout my life. I cannot wait to come home and dance with you again on the streets of heaven. I love and miss you both so very much.

My "special friend," my birdie in the wind: Knowing you are there in the background, praying and thinking of me every time I face another stepping-stone in the justice system, gives a power and determination to my journey I cannot describe in words.

My Daddy: I know I caused some sleepless nights. Thank you for always standing behind me, pushing me to want more and for teaching me the skills to survive in times of need. I miss you and love you daddy, rest in peace. Kiss my grammas for me!

My mother and stepdad (dad #2): Even when I did not think I wanted you there, you were, loving me through the rough spots and dusting me off in my frustrations. Thank you for always being there throughout my life.

My mentors, my warrior ladies, my soul sisters, Laura, Pastor Cindy, Pastor Lori, Lulu, Anaira, Seleta: Ladies, without the late-night phone calls, the hugs, the laughter, tears, the conversation and, most importantly, all the prayer and love, these pages would not have come together as easily as they have. I love you all truly, deeply, and uniquely!

Miss Paige, Mr. Arns: Thank you for all the help in putting the words together to flow easily on these pages. All the Glory goes to God for leading me to you both in this project.

My beautiful faith family, so many beautiful souls: Thank you for the love and support and most of all prayer. There are too many of you to list, but I love and cherish you all.

I love all of you that have helped me through this journey and thus far in my life. You have been a blessing to me and so many others along your path may the Lord shine on you always.

Dearest Beloved,

I want to be the first to offer a warm hug and smile on this journey you are about to take. Within the pages of my story, I pray that you will find healing and inspiration, and truly begin to understand the love only the Lord our God can give you. He will meet you in the quiet, dark, lonely, and even scary places of your life and will wrap you in safety, warmth, and love beyond explanation. All you need to do is cry out to Him.

Throughout my life, God has walked with me and carried me through some rough stuff. While my eyes were not always looking at Him, God was always right there watching me, waiting for me to reach out and take His strong, ever-loving outstretched hand and lean on Him alone as my protector, provider and one true love. My life has by no means been the ideal "perfect" life. I have made my share of mistakes—I am a sinner—but by the shed blood of Jesus Christ, all our sins are washed away. We are made new, fresh, and clean as new-fallen snow. I still make mistakes and tend to say or do the wrong thing at the wrong time, but by mercy and grace I can repent and walk on in forgiveness.

In the dark, quiet moments, He has come to me and led me to reach out and share my story in the hopes of healing others—not just women and girls, but men and families. He loves us all so deeply and purely it cannot be described in words. God has loved and pursued me throughout my entire life, but only within the last several years did I truly see it. I pray that throughout this book you find something that sparks a need in you to sit and listen in the quiet moments for God to speak to your heart in whatever situation you face. Healing from deep hurt, abuse, assault, and so many of life's storms is not by any means easy or tear-free, but let Christ romance you away from hate and unforgiveness, for these things are destructive to us and bear no weight for those who have sinned against us, despite what many of us believe. Let Christ hold you, dance with you, and play out what beautiful things He has in store for all of us.

Thank you for taking the time to seek Him and thank you for allowing my story to be a part of helping you with yours.

Walking beside you,
Deborah

I, Deborah
דבורה

I originally started to write this story out in 2011, still raw with emotions, but needing more time to heal, I put this project away, trying not to be discouraged. At the end of 2020 and into 2021, I was being led to "dig up the little stuff" left behind, deal with it, heal from it, and walk on in victory by completing this book for you.

God started a work in me from the day I was born. My name is that of a warrior and leader, a judge in the time when the judges, not kings, ruled Israel. My parents always made it quite clear that I was born for a purpose and a greatness. My namesake is found in the book of Judges in the Old Testament. Deborah's story starts at Judges 4:4. She stepped up and stepped in when no man would, and my father made sure I knew I was born of a warrior and leader's spirit. I remember reading the verse many times as a little girl with my dad. I always found it so fun, and it made my heart beat with pride that Deborah ruled in the mountains of the land of Ephraim. This was my Papa's name, Ephraim Albert. My dad's father was the only grandfather I really knew, as my mom's dad passed when I was still an infant. I remember thinking that being tied to my Papa like that was so special and that no one could ever take that gift from me.

> [4]*Now Deborah, a prophetess, the wife of Lapidoth, was judging Israel at that time.* [5]*And she would sit under the palm tree of Deborah between Ramah and Bethel in the mountains of Ephraim. And the children of Israel came up to her for judgment.*
> —*Judges 4:4–5, NKJV*

My childhood was average. I had a family that loved me and friends that I was close to. My parents were divorced when I was young, but my little brother and I never had to wonder where we stood. My parents always made sure we had what we needed and that we knew we were loved. I spent a lot of time with both my grandmothers as well. Not realizing what that would mean for me later in life, I did, however, cherish all the time I had with both. My dad's mother was a stay-at-home mother of an only son. She raced mini cars and was outspoken, all the while radiating strength and gentleness. My mom's mother was the wife of an Army Air Corps Colonel turned history teacher, and a mother of four. She was dedicated to her family, her church, and her community. Neither woman was weak in spirit. Both stood as strong pillars in the family and in their work in their communities. My mother still jokes about how both women could tell you off in such a way that would make you hug them and thank them on your way out the door. She frequently says it is a skill I was born with, inherited from them. They also exhibited a love and protectiveness of family and community.

I was in dance and gymnastics, and then joined the JROTC (Junior Reserve Officer Training Corps) in high school. I enjoyed horseback riding, and had the privilege of showing with my dad a few times, both in horse and dog arenas. I enjoyed many extracurricular activities from various sports, including swimming, to street dancing—a favorite of mine. I enjoyed my time with my friends and I read a lot. The outdoors is still my favorite place to be. Nothing beats the cool crisp air that flows through our beloved Rocky Mountains.

I was a decent student most of my life, only truly getting into trouble in high school, as most of us do while we try to find ourselves. Nothing major, just slipping grades and some ditched classes. Late in my junior year my two best friends at the time made the choice to leave school, and I chose to stay and finish. By this point, I had made the choice to enlist, but I had not decided which branch yet. I started JROTC in the middle of my junior year, initially to get out of gym class. I had no idea at the time the ride I was in for the next three semesters.

With friends off doing their own things and my career path chosen, I hunkered into school and busted out my last semester as a junior and the entirety of my senior year, seemingly making up for lost time. I became an "A" student again, and served on a student health committee that created a video for young girls on health. I became the nominee for the military ball queen for our school and won runner-up in the entire district. This specific competition was based on grades and community involvement—not so much on the popularity of your class, like prom royalty is. By then, I had made my decision to join the Marine Corps. I graduated that May the highest-ranked, most-decorated female cadet in my school's history at the time. I was also the only female to enlist in the Marine Corps from my high school's history, and the only enlistee to the Marines in two years.

In July I turned 18 and, come August 1st, away I went to Marine Corps Recruit Depot (MCRD) Parris Island, South Carolina. I served this beloved country for ten and a half years between active duty and reserve time. I have been all over the continental United States and was even stationed in Hawaii at one point.

I truly loved my time in the service. I have seen a ton of amazing things and been blessed by many experiences. I have made some of the most amazing friends and have suffered some heavy heartbreak. I have been humbled and honored by escorting several fallen brothers to their final resting places.

> [12]*This is My commandment, that you love one another as I have loved you.* [13]*Greater love has no one than this, than to lay down one's life for his friends.*
> —*John 15:12–13, NKJV*

Having completed both a secular college degree and a seminary training certification, I continue to have a thirst for knowledge. This has led me to take countless courses on nutrition and fitness, due to my own health issues. I have a newfound joy in the kitchen with various creations. Some of my favorite times now are just hanging out with my family, mixing up a batter of some sort to bake cookies, cinnamon rolls, or a casserole. Teaching my "little" to make my Dad's favorite chocolate-chip cookies was some of the most fun.

My life has been by no means perfect and 100% great all the time. There have been mistakes and failed relationships: Moves, projects started and never finished, fights with friends and family, leaving us months or more not speaking. In the end, through love and forgiveness on all sides, amends were made, wounds were healed, and life continued. Beloved, know that none of us is perfect; we all make mistakes. The Bible repeatedly reminds us gently of this fact.

> [10]*As it is written: "There is none righteous, no, not one. . ."*
> —*Romans 3:10, NKJV*

It is what you *do* with the mistakes you make that truly matters. Choose to learn and walk forward in the lessons; do not let them weigh you down with guilt and shame. Nothing you could ever do is unforgivable; you simply need to repent, ask for forgiveness, and turn from your mistakes. In Hebrew, the word is *shub* (pronounced "shoob"); one must turn and walk away from sin.

> *23for all have sinned and fall short of the glory of God, 24being justified freely by His grace through the redemption that is in Christ Jesus,*
>
> —*Romans 3:23–24, NKJV*

I am now extremely active in my community not too far from where I grew up. I enjoy my family and my friends greatly. I am blessed to lead a team of amazing people in an incredible charity for children. I enjoy riding motorcycles with my beloved and our friends and taking trips to explore this beautiful country. I love my faith family and the impact that we have on each other as we live this life together.

A trusted pastor I counseled with back in 2010 asked that I pray about writing a book on this story, my story. His reasoning was simple: in all his years in ministry, he counseled many of the offenders, yet very rarely the survivors. He had read many stories of survivors that walked away from God, survivors that had found God and survivors that had never, and still don't, know God. Yet he couldn't recall reading a single story from a survivor that leaned on and trusted God throughout her experience. I took that suggestion home and prayed for about a week. I asked God that, if this is what He truly wanted from me, He would give me a word to center this book around. Never failing, sitting at Noodles Restaurant alone one night writing a letter to my best friend Christopher, God gave me the word "Romance" as the theme to my story. A bit later on, as we walk through this together, I will explain in more detail. Yes, there is "His Divine Romance" all throughout my story, and there is in yours as well. A passionate pursuit by the Father chasing His beloved child.

Beloved, know that I understand not all who read this will have had the "normal" childhood and loving upbringing I had. I know that some of you have been through immense pain and abuse, have felt and been unloved for years. I was not led to write this book for any other purpose than to reach the hurting and to show you that whether you knew it then or not, or know it now or not, God has always been with you. He has always loved you and wanted nothing but the best for you. In your pain, in the midst of your battle, whatever it may be, He is there with you, He does love you no matter what!

Many of you have even questioned, and probably still do, "If He is so great and loving, why do these things happen to us?" I am here to tell you, not as a scolding mother or intimidating counselor, but as a loving girlfriend without judgment, that the Lord will not stop free will. He did not stop it for Adam and Eve in the garden and He will not stop the bad choices people make today, but He can and will carry us through it all. As a parent cannot stop the choice of a child who makes a bad choice in action, a parent can only hope that the child learns from the choice and comfort him in the aftermath. My story, I hope and pray, will give you the courage and the strength to dig deeper into your own story. I pray that you would cry out to God in your pain and your hurt and ask Him, "Where are You? You say I am loved; show me!" He will; this I promise you.

Our God is a gracious and loving Father who has literally written our stories in beautiful vast colors and victories. The enemy, satan, has fallen and seeks to destroy the beauty created in you. He is a deceiver and the ultimate liar, casting a falsehood upon everything God has created. I will show you examples of his clear deception in my story, though not always clear to me at the time. Just as with Adam and Eve in the Garden as they encounter the serpent, he will trick you and lie to you, and does it all in such subtle ways you can fall into a trap.

> [1]*Now the serpent was more cunning than any beast of the field which the Lord God had made. And he said to the woman, "Has God indeed said, 'You shall not eat of every tree of the garden'?"* [2]*And the woman said to the serpent, "We may eat the fruit of the trees of the garden;* [3]*but of the fruit of the tree which is in the midst of the garden, God has said, 'You shall not eat it, nor shall you touch it, lest you die.'"* [4]*Then the serpent said to the woman, "You will not surely die.* [5]*For God knows that in the day you eat of it your eyes will be opened, and you will be like God, knowing good and evil."*
>
> —*Genesis 3:1–5, NKJV*

We have all done it, we will do it many times over in our lives, but God is loving and just and as we cry out, He will come to our rescue.

> [17]*The righteous cry out and the Lord hears; and delivers them out of all their troubles.* [18]*The Lord is near those who have a broken heart, and saves such as have a contrite spirit.*
>
> —*Psalm 34:17–18, NKJV*

The Lord does not always work in our timing. He does not always give us what we think we need when we think we need it. My story will also show you examples of this. He works all things in perfect timing for you individually, connecting the family of faith He is building in each of us perfectly, in the timing that is right for our steps and best for His plans. I want you to remember this simple thought as you read these pages and think of your own story: *It is okay.* God is big enough. God is big enough for you to scream at, He is big enough for you to cuss at and yell at. You can shake your fists, pound the floor, have a temper tantrum. Our God is big enough to handle it all. The best part is that He is also big enough to hold you and love you unconditionally through it all. God is big enough to take all your pain and anger and tears and turn those ashes into beautiful diamonds of pure brilliance. He can and will turn the ugly from your hurt into the abundant, brilliant, beautiful you He has always intended you to be.

> [1] *The Spirit of the Lord God is upon Me, because the Lord has anointed Me to preach good tidings to the poor; He has sent me to heal the brokenhearted, to proclaim liberty to the captives, and the opening of the prison to those who are bound;* [2] *To proclaim the acceptable year of the Lord, and the day of vengeance of our God; to comfort all who mourn,* [3] *To console those who mourn in Zion, to give them beauty for ashes, the oil of joy for mourning, the garment of praise for the spirit of heaviness; that they may be called trees of righteousness, the planting of the Lord, that He may be glorified.*
> —Isaiah 61:1–3 NKJV

Strength in History

Mabel Jane Shefferd Hust and Janet Mary Burnham Wenger are the two most influential women in my history. These women *stood* out without *sticking* out; they were solid in faith and strength. They loved their families and served their communities. It took a traumatic event, a lot of pain, tears, and 33 years to realize the impact they had on my life.

Mabel was my father's mother. She was married to Ephraim Albert "Al" Hust in the early 1940s. They adopted a son, born in 1945: my dad, Eugene Roger. They lived in north Denver, and then Seattle for a while, before moving back to Colorado. My grandmother was active in the Catholic Church and served on several committees within its walls. I remember stories of how she raced mini cars at the old Lakeside Track off Sheridan and Interstate 70, supporting my dad in one of his hobbies. She baked: my favorite was her zucchini bread; the smell of her kitchen in the fall was so sweet and delicious.

Mabel was devoted to my grandfather; I called him Papa and my Daddy all her days.

One of my favorite examples of her strength is when my dad was middle-school-aged. My grandmother—quite outspoken as to the ways women, and especially mothers, were treated in the church—at one point raised such a stink that the Archbishop of Denver himself asked her to leave the parish she was part of. She could not be silenced about her feelings of inequality. My grandmother did not mind hard work and did not even really want the credit or recognition for it either, but she was not going to stand for women and mothers getting walked on and ignored for their service and sacrifices for the community and their families. The church apparently took issue with that. In that meeting with the leadership, she let them know exactly how she felt in an ever-so-ladylike and appropriate manner. Then, when they asked her to either comply with their rules and her place within the parish or leave, she said, "Thank you very much!", and left without looking back.

She continued racing minis and supporting my Papa and Daddy in everything they did and helping other moms in the community with baskets of needs and home-baked goods. My grandma was sweet and kind, but a force to be reckoned with. When my little brother and I came along, her whole world would shift from my Papa and my dad to now four of us, who completed her joy. We took trips together, baked cakes and cookies, went swimming, spent weekends. She even had a salad that was the very first dish she ever taught me how to make. I loved it so much she wrote the recipe out and titled it: "Debbie Goo." My two favorite trips were to Disneyland in California when I was in the fourth grade and getting to spend my 13th birthday at the top of the Space Needle in Seattle, Washington, with Grandma's sister Nell.

My Grandma Hust would brush my hair and tell me always how I was destined for great things and that there was a fire in me I should never let anyone put out. She taught me how to be a lady, and always insisted on manners and proper etiquette. I learned to cook and bake from her; I learned how to set a formal dining table and entertain guests of any number, in any genre. I still enjoy so much of that today. Being surrounded by family and friends at a barbecue or formal holiday celebration is absolutely my favorite thing to do.

She and my grandfather met while they worked at the Brown Palace Hotel in the historic district of downtown Denver. Papa was the head maître d', known as the Ship's Captain at the Ship's Tavern in the main lobby of the hotel, and Grandma was head of housekeeping. Her primary duties were to supervise the maids and teach etiquette to the servers in the restaurant. The Brown Palace is still part of downtown Denver's most elite stops. It has housed presidents and various other diplomats over the years. I even have the letter written to my Papa from former President Dwight D. Eisenhower, personally thanking him for the hospitality to him and his staff in a visit to Denver. My grandparents were always an amazing example of faith and humility in service.

My Grandma Hust taught me that in the face of oppression, I should stand solid in faith and know that I am someone, made for a purpose, whether those I faced thought so or not. Little did I know those seeds she planted would bloom and that her words would ring in my ears over and over in the worst moments of my life. They would become repetitious words that would carry me through darkness and bring out the fight in me. My Grandma Hust went home to Jesus on January 5th of my senior year of high school. She was laid to rest next to my Papa in North Denver, not too far from where they raised my Daddy.

Janet was my mother's mother. She was married to Robert Marion Wenger in the early 1930s. They had four children: two girls and two boys. My mother Cecelia Marie was the third. Robert was a pilot in the Army Air Corps in WWII who retired a Colonel. He was respectfully called "The Colonel" by many in our family, and went on to teach history with the Adams County School District in northeast Denver. My grandfather had even authored the high school history book that was, at one point, taught throughout the district, and Janet served her community, all while raising four children. She was very active in the Methodist Church. Gramma helped start, and also served in, a low-income community housing program designed to help families become self-sufficient from government assistance. This community, still active and a blessing to many to this day, gave families their own apartment, had job resources and my grandmother taught the children in the onsite school they provided. Janet was very much a "watcher," if you will, and she was extremely sweet and outgoing, but she was not as readily vocal as my other grandmother.

My favorite memories of her strength were her steadfastness in her Bible studies and church activities. Nothing could keep my grandmother from attending choir practice, Bible studies, craft sales, and community dinners. You could always find her there at the church, serving, smiling, and hugging. As she aged, her knees became an issue and mobility was hard, but every chance she got, she served. The only people she was more devoted to than those of her church family and friends, were her children and grandchildren, of which there are six. I am the fifth grandchild and the last girl. My grandmother always loved having my cousins in town over the summers so that we could all spend time together and have big family time, either out to dinner or at home, ordering pizza.

My Gramma Wenger used to let me curl up on her lap to watch old sitcoms and cartoons, or she would read to me. If I were sad or hurt myself playing, I could put my head in her lap and she would stroke my hair, tell me how much she and Jesus loved me and either sing or hum to me. She always chose the tune of *Jesus Loves Me* when she would hum. My Gramma's favorite song to sing when we were together was *The Rose*. When she was sick in the hospital, I would go visit a lot on my own after school, before going home and coming back with the family. Even though the doctors said she could not hear me, I always sang her *The Rose* and I stroked her hair and told her how much Jesus and I loved her. When she went home to Jesus on January 6th of my junior year, it was the hardest loss I had ever dealt with at that point in my life.

I had lost an aunt who was one of my mom's dear friends, two grandfathers, and a beloved neighbor all of us kids called "Grampa Joe," but losing my Gramma Wenger was the most difficult, and I never quite understood why until now. She taught me Jesus' love. She did not just read us Scripture and take us to church; she *lived* His love. She never met a stranger; she always had time for her family, especially her grandkids. Janet exemplified peace and unconditional love. We never had to doubt where we stood with her; each one of us was special in our own unique way. She did not have much to give us in going places or physical gifts, but she spoiled us in time and love. When I had a bad day at school from a bad test grade or a mean kid on the playground, I was always so at peace when I got to talk to or see my Gramma. My Gramma was always the one who stayed with us when my little brother or I was home sick from school. She made the best Campbell's Chicken Soup. It came from a can, sure, but somehow Gramma made it the best.

In these revelations throughout my healing, it became quite clear to me why, that day at Ft. Logan, I collapsed at her headstone, in her lap, and cried like a little girl: I had my peace, I had my Gramma. I have learned since then to always cherish any time you have with those dearest to you. I am so grateful that neither of my grandmothers were alive here on earth when I was assaulted, but I am so grateful they were my grandmothers, for the strength and life-lessons in love they gave me are what helped my faith walk, so I knew Who to lean on and where to turn in the dark moments. *Jesus!* I always thought I was so much like my Daddy and that I got everything from him. I *am* like him—he was my best friend—but all the woman of faith that I am came from the two most beautiful souls anyone could have ever been blessed with: my grandmothers.

Mabel and Janet, I love you Grandma and Gramma. Thank you both so much for everything!

³. . .the older women likewise, that they be reverent in behavior, not slanderers, not given to much wine, teachers of good things— ⁴that they admonish the young women to love their husbands, to love their children, ⁵to be discreet, chaste, homemakers, good, obedient to their own husbands, that the word of God may not be blasphemed.
—Titus 2:3–5, NKJV

The Rose

Some say love, it is a river, that drowns the tender reed;
Some say love, it is a razor, that leaves your soul to bleed;
Some say love, it is a hunger, an endless aching need;
I say love, it is a flower, and you, its only seed.

It's the heart afraid of breaking, that never learns to dance;
It's the dream afraid of waking, that never takes the chance;
It's the one who won't be taking, who cannot seem to give;
And the soul afraid of dying, that never learns to live.

When the night has been too lonely and the road has been too long,
And you think that love is only for the lucky and the strong,
Just remember in the winter, far beneath the bitter snows
Lies the seed, that with the sun's love in the spring becomes the rose.

Written by: Amanda McBroom
Lyrics © Warner Chappell Music, Inc.
Lyrics Licensed & Provided by LyricFind
Originally Performed by Bette Midler: *The Divine Miss M*

Jesus Loves Me

Jesus loves me, this I know,
For the Bible tells me so.
Little ones to Him belong;
They are weak, but He is strong.

> *Yes, Jesus loves me,*
> *Yes, Jesus loves me,*
> *Yes, Jesus loves me,*
> *The Bible tells me so.*

Jesus loves me—He who died
Heaven's gate to open wide.
He will wash away my sin,
Let His little child come in.

> *Yes, Jesus loves me,*
> *Yes, Jesus loves me,*
> *Yes, Jesus loves me,*
> *The Bible tells me so.*

> *Yes, Jesus loves me,*
> *Yes, Jesus loves me,*
> *Yes, Jesus loves me,*
> *The Bible tells me so.*

Please enjoy these photos, as I put faces to the names of those mentioned that mean the most to me. . .

My Dad: E.R. Hust, Sr.

Like Father

Like Daughter

Christopher

Robyn

Grandma Mabel and Papa Ephraim
(Daddy's Mama and Dad)

Grandma Janet and The Colonel, Robert
(Mom's Mama and Dad)

My Boaz: Robert "Preach"

The Enemy Appears

Beloved, the enemy, satan, strikes us when we are in our lowest, most un-suspecting moments. Even when we feel as though we are pushing through, he finds the weak point and strikes. To comparatively visualize, look into nature. While God has created these beautiful creatures, there is an advisory to all living beings. The eagle or the hawk does not swoop into a field full of rabbits and mice and pluck out the largest and strongest to take for food. The bird of prey watches, circles, and waits for the lone, or the lame, weak prey. The wolf waits for the lost sheep, the lioness for the slowest antelope. The snake slithers on the ground, and then coils in hiding, until its prey unsus-pectedly walks right up to it and is struck with a quick, sharp, and often deadly bite.

The Lord has created us all as relational humans. We need relationship to function. His design is for us to be in a key relationship with Him above all. We are lonely and at a weak point when we are out of relationship, whether we realize it or not. When we lose a loved one, lose contact with a friend, lose a job, whatever the reasons, when we lose relationship, we become a perfect target for the enemy to attack. Even if we do not feel the loss is sig-nificant, there is a void that must be grieved for. In this moment, I want to take you back to the most significant loss of relationship in my life, when I lost more than just my daddy, but extended family and friends. The point where I was weakest, even though I felt I was handling it well, was just after my stepfamily and several close friends turned their backs on me shortly after my dad's passing. The issue was *I* was handling it; I did not allow God to come in and protect and heal the way only He can.

In April of 2009, my dad and best friend of 32 years passed away. I was at peace with the fact that he was no longer suffering or in pain and that he was at home, healed and strong again. I had been blessed in the last several months of his life to grow closer to him than we had ever been. He and my stepmom had moved over from the western slope of Colorado to just east of Pueblo, so they were much closer. We took walks, talked every day and I would see them almost every weekend. My most memorable moments where when he was in the hospital and then hospice, he would ask me to read to him, mostly from the Bible, sometimes whatever chapter I was in from the current book I was reading. Yet we always went back to the Bible. Daddy's favorite verse was Matthew 11:28, "Come to me all who are weary, and I will give you rest." He'd lay back, close his eyes, and say, "Read me the one about rest, baby. I am tired, and I need to rest. Read me that one." We would also recite the Lord's Prayer and Psalm 23, but Matthew was daddy's favorite.

> *28 Come to Me, all you who labor and are heavy laden, and I will give you rest. 29 Take My yoke upon you and learn from Me, for I am gentle and lowly in heart, and you will find rest for your souls. 30 For My yoke is easy and My burden is light.*
> —Matthew 11:28–30, NKJV

Daddy had left me in charge of his will and papers (not a fair thing for a daughter when there is a wife involved), but he honestly did not trust my step-family and wanted to make sure I was taken care of and that my brother had access to some of his things. I lodged the will and tried to be a team player, fair about all things, quickly discovering that all the warnings about watching my back while he was alive were well warranted. My stepfamily was contin-uously going behind my back, trying to close accounts and access monies and property my dad had without the proper permissions from the state, according to his last will and testament. They constantly threw such phrases at me like "Your precious daddy never loved you like you think he did. You were just a necessary thing for him to tolerate." or "Where is my money? You don't de-serve this. You did nothing for him; you weren't even there when he died!" I remember well the last time I spoke to my stepbrother. I very bluntly and coldly said, "My dad wasn't a paycheck and I'd gladly give it all to you to have him back for five minutes. This is over, and I will not tolerate this behavior any more!" I hung up and have not spoken to any of them since that moment.

At one point I even received a phone call from the attorney I had hired to help my dad update his will, informing me that my stepfamily was trying to find an attorney to represent them as they sue me for all my dad's estate. He assured me that they had no grounds, as I am blood heir and the named executor of the estate, but that if they did find an attorney dumb enough to take their case, he would happily represent me for free, just to put them in their place. Beloved, see this now for what it was: God's oversight for His daughter—me—and protection in a battle.

Death does do weird things to families and causes needless stress and fights. I tried to write off the stress and attitudes of my stepmom and stepbrother to grief. It worked for a while, but it then became evident I was not a welcome presence in the family anymore, evident by the continuously hurtful things that were said and done. I picked myself up, dusted off, and quickly washed my hands of them, saying to myself and others I trusted that I am not the one to answer for their attitudes on Judgment Day; that is for God to deal with. I stopped speaking to both in late May of 2009.

Feeling confident that I was standing solid and able to move on, I was attacked yet again. I had been working with a youth group for over six years and had fought several times to keep our group afloat. I would have done anything for these kids. All my free time was focused on this group. There were several women on staff with me that for some reason decided it was time for me to go. Accusations were made against me that were in no way true. People I thought were solid would not even hear me out or see the paperwork I had to support "my side" of the story. I had made mistakes, sure, but nothing like these accusations. Knowing I had not done anything wrong and having all the hard paper evidence to prove it, I walked away from them as well, washing my hands and giving it to God like I did with my stepfamily. In times of trial, you find out who is truly with you and who is not. They created such a stir that it took several months to completely be free of them.

Picking up and dusting off again, very proud of myself for the way I was handling the death of my dad, loss of friends as well as family, I found quickly that when you feel solid, you truly are in the middle of quicksand. In the weakness and pain of losing my father, the enemy struck and derailed a plan God had predestined for my life. That, beloved, is what he tries to do. He lies in wait, like a predator or a snake waiting for the weak to walk by, and then he strikes. Sometimes he strikes hard and fast, and sometimes it is a slow, subtle attack on your soul.

In September of 2009 I went to a Marine Corps League function. We were welcoming home a wounded Marine who had lost his legs in Iraq. The Patriot Guard Motorcycle Association was also there at the request of the family. I met him that day. I met the enemy in the flesh, a large teddy bear of flesh named Kirk.

Standing for a group picture, we were all squeezed together to fit in the frame. I was placed right next to him. Something shifted in me. I felt the desire to flirt and banter back and forth with him. I thought it was okay just to flirt a bit, make a new friend, maybe go for a motorcycle ride, or just hang out. From that moment on, Kirk pursued me in such a fiercely passionate way. He appeared to hang on my every word and pay attention to my every need and desire. I fell in love with him fast and hard. He was a former men's motorcycle ministry leader and choir member in church. He read to me every night, even over the phone, cooked for me, prayed with me. He was everything I thought I ever wanted. The enemy has and will counterfeit everything the Lord has and does, to deceive and trap his prey.

> [14]*And no wonder! For Satan himself transforms himself into an angel of light.* [15]*Therefore it is no great thing if his ministers also transform themselves into ministers of righteousness, whose end will be according to their works.*
> —2 Corinthians 11:14–15, NKJV

A few short weeks in, Kirk came over one night and said he needed to share some things with me and that they might change my mind about being with him. I expected something serious and devastating, like he had cancer or some other illness. Instead, what he had to tell me was that he had served a little time in California for a misunderstanding between him and a former girlfriend. She had made accusations against him that were untrue and had what he called "buyer's remorse." They had been drinking and wound up sleeping together. I had heard several stories like this before. Girls that had drunk a little too much at a party and slept with a guy they barely knew, then tried to appease a boyfriend or parent by accusing the young man of assaulting them. I had even had an acquaintance in high school make such an accusation and had a young man's life almost destroyed because of it. Besides, this big ol' teddy bear of a man had already proven how sweet, gentle, and Christian he was, hadn't he?

> [3]*But I fear, lest somehow, as the serpent deceived Eve by his craftiness, so your minds may be corrupted from the simplicity that is in Christ.* [4]*For if he who comes preaches another Jesus whom we have not preached, or if you receive a different spirit which you have not re-*

ceived, or a different gospel which you have not accepted—you may well put up with it!
—2 Corinthians 11:3–4, NKJV

After we talked for several hours and he even cried on my shoulder, he held me while we slept. That was the first night we had ever spent together. Though nothing sexual happened that night, the desire was there. Kirk had insisted it was too soon in our courtship and he had too much respect for me to have sex just yet.

At his request, I had made the decision to break off a long deep-rooted friendship with Christopher, my best friend of just over six years. Kirk had also talked me into severing ties with Christopher's family as well, stating that if I was going to pursue this relationship with him, I should be completely free and clear of my past. At the time, this made perfect sense to me. Devastating my best friend, offering very little explanation, I ended everything with Christopher. Our years of friendship were done. Being the man I always knew him to be, through his tears and pain, Christopher stated all he ever wanted was my happiness and wished me well. Later that night I ended my long-time friendship with his mother and brothers as well. These would not be the last relationships Kirk tried very hard to take from me.

The following week we went out to dinner. In what I thought to be the most romantic way possible, Kirk asked for commitment, though not yet ready to marry due to wounds of the past. We were at Chili's Bar & Grill eating dinner and he kept pushing me in a playful way to hurry up and finish, telling me all the while he wanted to take me some place special, somewhere he was sure I had never been. When I did finally finish my dinner, we sat there at the table just talking for a bit. I told him I was ready to go to this place. He smiled and said let us just sit for a minute and take in this moment. Just then the manager and entire staff came around the corner with a chocolaty dessert and looked like they were about to sing happy birthday to someone. They stopped at our table. The next thing I knew they had placed the plate down in front of me and in caramel it read "Deb, will you. . ." I looked to Kirk, who at this time was on his knees as he finished, ". . .be mine?" I started to cry. I said yes. After all, I was falling in love with him. He cried too, while the manager, staff, and the rest of the patrons cheered. On the way out, he danced with me all the way to the car. My head was spinning out of control in a whirlwind of emotions. He had not even met my parents yet!

The night after Chili's, we went to meet with some friends of mine from the Marine Corps League (MCL). Sitting with one of my trusted girlfriends,

39

also a former Marine, she cautioned me that maybe it was a little fast after losing my dad, but she was happy for me and just wanted me to be careful and happy. I called my mother and stepdad and asked them to meet us for lunch. I wanted them to meet Kirk. We had lunch on a Saturday, and afterwards he surprised me by taking me to a little park area nestled in the foothills within Red Rocks Park. The area was beautiful and perfect. It would to be "our spot" for picnics and afternoon retreats. A place for just us. Maybe someday even more.

December came, and everything was going smoothly in this new level of "love." His daughter had flown in from Alaska for the holidays and all was just wonderful. On the 20th of December, we shared a breakfast with a few friends and family in Golden and then headed to church. The day was perfect. We spent the night away just the two of us in a hotel just outside of Golden, nothing fancy, just away from the norm, our first Christmas together. Life was beginning to look absolutely "perfect."

It took me thirty-three years to finally understand He loves me no matter what and answers prayer from the heart. Throughout the rest of this story, I will walk you step by step through the mercy and grace of our beloved Lord and Savior. In the moments of question when anyone could ask, "Where was God in that?" it will be my pleasure, beloved, to share with you exactly where He was in all of it. He will never leave us or forsake us; He has even promised us that in writing. Jesus has held me in His mighty arms and has shielded me in the darkest moments.

> ⁵*No man shall be able to stand before you all the days of your life; as I was with Moses, so I will be with you. I will never leave you or forsake you.*
>
> —*Joshua 1:5, NKJV*

Just briefly, let me take you back to my dad's last days. As I said in the beginning, he was my best friend. Like many children do, I took my dad—*both* my parents, really—for granted most of my teenage and early adult life. I needed my daddy as a little girl and I needed him as a woman, but in all the middle stuff, he gave me the grace to fall on my face. He always answered the phone but did not always run to the rescue. The night he told me he was sick, I was in shock. This is my Superman; what do you mean you're dying? He had developed cirrhosis of the liver and later developed liver cancer. My dad was a functioning alcoholic and had his faults for sure, but he is the one who taught me survival skills, practiced my gymnastics with me, built me doll houses, taught me to shoot and handle various weapons, work on cars, and cook. He taught me quite a bit. He was never abusive or hateful—firm in discipline, but never hateful and angry. My dad was Navy, then Law Enforcement, so naturally I considered the military and ultimately decided on the Marine Corps. Also, an ordained minister, my dad was key in my faith in Christ.

I knew about Daddy's illness for about three or three and a half years. Every chance I got to see him, I took. I could not believe I was losing the one person I was always able to lean on no matter what. I argued with God, I fought with Him. I even got quite angry several times. Yet, all the while, He was there, standing strong, loving me through it. I, of course, could not see it at the time, but God was there in every car ride to visit, on the phone with every phone call. He was right there.

At the end of his life here on earth, my dad and I were blessed to spend a lot of time together in the hospital and at hospice care. He would ask me to read Scripture to him and would talk to me about what I thought heaven would be like. He would "rally" every time I came to see him. It got to be so difficult on the family—the ups and downs: he could go now, no, wait, he is still with us. Oh, it was hard. I remember going home one night about a week or two before he died and falling to my knees in the living room, just screaming and crying like a two-year-old. "God, You are the healer, so heal him! Either take him home or heal him here, but I cannot fight this fight for him anymore! Just move! I give up! Just *do* something! It's all on You!!!" I am sure my roommate thought I was losing my mind a bit.

The next time I went to see Daddy was a few days later. I sat on the bed with him in his nursing-home room and asked him why he would not go home. He smiled and said, "If I go, baby, who will take care of you?" I told him I would be fine, and he just shook his head in disbelief. He pointed at two pictures I had given him of the two people closest to me: Christopher and Robyn. I took them down and handed them to him. He took the picture of Chris and placed his hand over Chris' face. He sat silent for a minute and then grabbed my hand and prayed silently with me. It was like Daddy knew: Christopher would step in for him as my family. When finished, he looked up at me and said, "Okay, I will go; He is calling me home." Five days later, Daddy passed away. I was sleeping on the couch at home that night and woke up to use the restroom. When I came back, I just sat back against the couch, almost like I was resting against someone. There came a deep sigh of relief, an exhale I cannot explain, and a sudden peace. About fifteen minutes later, my stepmom called to tell me Daddy had died. I said I knew, I just felt it, I told her I loved her and laid down to the most peaceful sleep I had had in months.

The next morning, I woke up, got dressed, packed a bag, and headed south from Greeley. During the drive down, I made the necessary phone calls: my mother and stepdad, my boss, Christopher, Robyn, and a few others. I got to my older stepbrother's house and we waited for my stepmom there. I was in that "what needs done, let's do it" mode. The last several months of preparation were about to unfold in ways I would not have expected.

For months, my father had warned me about not trusting my stepfamily and that I needed to watch my back. He had said on several occasions if he felt he had the fight and the time left, he would have left and filed for divorce. I put it all in the back of my mind and hoped my dad was wrong and just speaking from illness. I humored him, though, and helped him update his estate papers and hired a lawyer for him and myself, just in case. Unfortunately, he was not wrong. Almost instantly the daggers started coming at me full force. We had to fight about everything.

Death does strange things to people: whether it is their grief or true colors, only they will ever know. I had a strange peace about ending a 20-plus-year relationship with that part of my family. My Dad prepared me by warning me, and God allowed my overall grief to include releasing their relationships as well as my dad's. The grieving process we must go through to heal is not just for death, but for any hurts, pains, or losses in life that we experience. Once you can understand that and know that God has designed it to take place through steps and various levels of emotion, you can rest easy that He will walk you through all of it, through answered or seemingly unanswered prayers, through people and, most importantly, in the quiet times when it is just you, your thoughts, your pain, and God.

> [23] *Nevertheless, I am continually with You; You hold me by my right hand.* [24] *You will guide me with your counsel, and afterward receive me to glory.*
>
> —*Psalm 73:23–24, NKJV*

The enemy is a coward and will do all he can to destroy what God has intended for you. God is the hero and redeemer and is always there to rescue and restore. While the plans He has in place for me have been derailed and delayed, the Lord will still see that they are carried out, for *He* is the author of our lives, not the cowardly enemy. A perfect example of this is the story of Job in the Bible. Job had everything taken from him and still he trusted all would be restored by the God who loved him. God did just as Job had believed, He restored everything, and God restored it bigger and more fruitful that Job had hoped. He will do the same for us. God will restore and heal all that has been destroyed. All He asks us to do is trust Him to do so.

I have told friends and confidants that, at times throughout this experience, I almost felt like Job. Almost as if God and Satan were in a discussion about me at the gates. Satan tells God that he believes I am not the person God knows me to be: I make far too many mistakes and have far too much sin to truly love and lean on God. In return, God says, "I know you are wrong. She loves me wholeheartedly no matter what." Satan offers a retort, "Well if you think so, how about letting me test her?" God, being all-knowing, replies, "Alright, as I know my daughter loves Me. Do whatever you want, just don't take her physical life." So it began.

> *6Now there was a day when the sons of God came to present themselves before the Lord, and Satan also came among them. 7And the Lord said to Satan, "From where do you come?" So Satan answered the Lord and said, "From going to and fro on the earth, and from walking back and forth on it." 8Then the Lord said to Satan, "Have you considered My servant Job, that there is none like him on the earth, a blameless and upright man, one who fears God and shuns evil?" 9So Satan answered the Lord and said, "Does Job fear God for nothing? 10Have You not made a hedge around him, around his household, and around all that he has on every side? You have blessed the work of his hands, and his possessions have increased in the land. 11But now, stretch out Your hand and touch all that he has, and he will surely curse You to Your face!" 12And the Lord said to Satan, "Behold, all that he has is in your power; only do not lay a hand on his person." So Satan went out from the presence of the Lord.*
>
> *—Job 1:6–12, NKJV*

Master at Deception

As the enemy often does, almost immediately—the *next day*—Kirk changed. It was like I was now his *property,* and not his partner. He questioned all that I did, kept tabs on me to and from work, criticized what I wore, monitored who I spoke with and when. Everything I did was under a microscope. He utilized Scripture to torment me into submission. He would constantly berate me with how I was supposed to cleave to my husband and leave my mother, and we weren't even married. One of his personal favorites to twist was in 1 Timothy: women were supposed to be silenced and seen, but not heard or noticed. I promise you, beloved, this is taken *way* out of context, which is what the enemy does. I encourage you to read the entire chapter.

> [9]In like manner also, that the women adorn themselves in modest apparel, with propriety and moderation, not with braided hair or gold or pearls or costly clothing, [10]but, which is proper for women professing godliness, with good works. [11]Let a woman learn in silence with all submission. [12]And I do not permit a woman to teach or to have authority over a man, but to be in silence. [13]For Adam was formed first, then Eve.
>
> —1 Timothy 2:9–13, NKJV

What was intended in this verse by a loving Father is that His daughters do not adorn themselves with too much bling and fancy clothes, so that their natural beauty, the beauty we were born with, is seen as primary, not makeup, jewels, and fancy clothes. The natural beautiful us, that is what God wants the world to see. In not having an authority over man is about not trying to control him and a man having authority over his wife is not intended for control, but for protection. Christ is our authority and in that He protects us from and through harm and bears the weight of our mistakes. Likewise, was the intention for man and woman. The man is to submit to Christ, answering for his wife in authority, for if she falls, the husband falls. A husband is to be willing to die for his wife, die to sin, die to self, and protect his wife's honor and life, as Christ protected His bride the church and died for us all. He created us all in His sight to be admired and cherished, not flaunted and controlled.

Kirk controlled me. He monitored my conversations with my mother and best friend Robyn, insisting all the while that Robyn was not a true follower of Christ. Robyn loves to remind us by gentle conversation what an entire verse says and that the Lord is love and not control or judgment. Robyn is also very fun-loving and full of joy. In short, she is beautifully silly. He harassed me about the fact that her Christmas gift was so late, knowing that she has Multiple Sclerosis and deals with memory issues. I came to a point where I just would not speak to her, or about her, with him around. I walked on eggshells about everything, learning quickly what did and did not set him off. As long as he was happy and I let him "run the show," life was peaceful. The second I questioned anything or stepped outside his box, all hell broke loose. The emotional and spiritual abuse was the worst of it all, though the verbal was harsh at times too. I remember getting to the point where I would just pray he would hit me, because bruises, cuts, and broken bones heal much more quickly than verbal and spiritual wounds.

About three weeks into our newly committed relationship and his new reign of control, I started praying quietly at night for God to show me something new. This was not His design for relationship and there had to be a way out, either through the front door or through counseling. My survival instincts started to kick in around then. Being a Marine and the daughter of a cop, I set up a prepaid cell phone I left in my desk at work, checked in with friends via email, and had mail sent to my office and even spoke with my immediate supervisor who still is a trusted friend. As the eggshells at home got increasingly difficult to maneuver, I reached out to Christopher. I wrote him a letter telling him very plainly if he never wanted to speak to me again, I would totally understand, but I did not know where else to turn. I needed prayer and support and I needed it right then. I had already shared my turmoil with Robyn, and she was standing firm by my side no matter the outcome. Christopher responded almost immediately, asking what was going on and what he could do. All I needed at that point was prayer and love. I shared the highlights of what I was dealing with at home and told him I did not know what was to come of this mess, but I was waiting on God to show me something—anything.

God did grant me the grace to ease my own life into peace, into shalom. "Shalom" in Hebrew is not only a greeting, but it also describes peace and harmony to the soul. The nastier Kirk got when we fought, the quicker I became silent and in prayer. There were times he would throw temper tantrums like a three-year-old and not take his medications for his heart and diabetes. By the strength given me, I still set them out every morning and every night with a glass of water and his cup for tea. I would even leave a note most times that just said, "I love you." I thought that with these new defense mechanisms, I could make it through this. I just became more and more controlled and watched by him.

In late February and early March of 2010, when it looked as if I would finally have the opportunity to leave him, I was laid off from my job due to economic cutbacks. Talk about a "whoa, wait a second" moment! I was devastated, not having a clue what I would do with no freedom and no money, but my supervisor agreed to allow me to still receive mail at the office, and I left all my important documents and the alternate cell phone there, and was able to keep my key. Again, in a moment of time, God stepped in to protect His child, allowing me a safety net to keep resources hidden from the enemy. Kirk appeared very sympathetic to the loss of my job and even suggested we attend a "Weekend To Remember" conference in Colorado Springs, a Family Life Ministry Christian conference, since it would help us to strengthen our relationship as a couple. Maybe we could find help and growth. What was I going to say, completely at his mercy? I told him that would be a great idea.

That weekend was an incredibly tense and stressful time. When we first arrived, I familiarized myself with the hotel and some of the staff of the conference. I met a woman there I just felt safe around. Kirk said he was not feeling well and went to lay down, asking me if I would get us dinner from the restaurant. I agreed, seeing a perfect opportunity to reach out to this woman I had seen. I sent him to the room and ordered dinner. While I was waiting for the food, I walked over to this woman and introduced myself, and just started to cry a bit. I told her I was not sure where or how to reach out, but things were not good at home and this was a last-ditch effort. She suggested a book to me about domestic violence in the church and said they would get a copy mailed to my mother's address. Apologies, my beloved: I cannot remember the title of the book. She also reassured me that God did not design abuse and control to be a key in relationship, and it was okay to get out and get safe, and then try to work things out if that was what was to happen. She hugged me and prayed with me, and then I took dinner back to Kirk in the room.

We had an intense night of awakenings in the seminar. Back in the room we fought, and he chose to sleep in the extra bed in the room, trying to punish me. I cried and prayed most of the night, getting up in the morning and getting ready for the day's seminars. Kirk rolled over and opted not to go. I kissed him on the shoulder and said I would come back at lunch to check on him, but he did not respond. Same thing at lunch: he stayed behind; I went. As part of the conference, we were to have a date night that Saturday night and have "bonding time." Surprisingly, he was up and dressed. He took me out for dinner and then to a movie, not saying a word the entire night. Then Sunday morning, he told me we were leaving. I said I wanted to stay and finish the conference. He dropped me off at the door and said he would be back for me.

Having spent the weekend alone, I just wanted to find that woman and tell her I was leaving. She met me in the prayer room and comforted me with some of the other staff; they talked me into staying for the women-only talk, offering me a ride all the way back to Denver if necessary. While I was in that room, Kirk apparently came into the back of the men-only talk and listened to the men speaking in their session. We met in the hall after both sessions and hugged for quite a while. He apologized and kissed me. I did not know what to think; was this for real or was it another one of his shows for the public eye? I thought I would just make the best of it and go with the good for now, since life had been so insane these last few months. He was back to how he was when we first courted. We had a great day the rest of the day. On the way home, we went to tour the Seven Falls, a natural area just outside Colorado Springs. The next day was even great.

Tuesday of that week I received a job lead from my recent supervisor: her cousin was hiring in accounting and she recommended me. I interviewed and got the job. Not realizing it at the time, I know now this job was given to me by God to allow me the ability to get out. It offered stability, support, and a bunch of prayer warriors. I started the week before Palm Sunday that March and loved it instantly. Kirk, having lost control of me during the day was not so thrilled, although he put on a great front for the community to see. But at home behind closed doors, he would berate me and yell at me about the long hours and schedule I would have.

Palm Sunday, March 28th, 2010, we were on the way to church. He was in one of his moods, upset about the way I was dressed in my turtleneck, jeans, and V-neck sweater. To him, I was not conservative enough. While normally I just shut down and quietly prayed my way through the demeaning and belittling comments he made, this time was different. As he started to drag out Scripture, I cut him off and snapped at him, "What would you have me do, wear a burlap sack or just stay locked away in the house? I can't help that God gave me the body He gave me!" That did it. He looked at me in such a rage I thought for sure I was done. He punched the steering wheel while driving at a high rate of speed on the highway. Breathing heavily and uneasy, I started to shake, asking God to get us to safety. He shouted that we were not going to church and pulled off the highway and into a parking lot. He told me if I wanted to go I could, but he was going home. He got out and slammed the door shut. I quickly locked the doors and sat there for a minute, trying to compose myself. I drove home and called my mother and stepdad. I was done. I was leaving that day.

While waiting for my parents, Kirk came home and proceeded to yell at me for leaving him behind and just driving off. I tried to explain that I did not see him, that I was too upset, and that he had frightened me. He lashed back at me verbally. It was then I got up the nerve to tell him I was leaving, just as my parents were pulling up. Kirk begged me not to go, putting on quite the convincing show. The more he begged, the more I prayed for God to keep me strong and get me out. He kept impeding my leaving, by standing in my way and blocking the door. My parents called the police for what is called a "civil standby." Two officers showed up and asked Kirk to leave for a while; he agreed, so they left. Kirk, of course, did not leave, so my stepdad had to call the police again. This time they stayed until he pulled away from the house and gave me two hours to leave. Collecting as much as I could in my car and my parents' car, I packed and left. Going by an ATM to withdraw a small amount of money for the week, the ATM took my card. I had no access to my money until banks opened Monday morning. My parents put me in a hotel that night and paid for a week to give me a few days to get some banking situated and my thoughts together. Crying, they left me there at the hotel.

Kirk called and asked if we could meet. He was sorry and wanted to discuss the space I needed and the counseling he wanted. Still under his spell and in complete shock, I agreed. I met him at Red Robin for dinner. We talked and had dinner. I did not mention where I was staying. He offered to put me up in a hotel for the night. I agreed, intending to check out as soon as he left me there. He also gave me a few dollars in cash since he was not sure why my card was taken when I tried to get money from the ATM earlier. We finished dinner and he followed me over to a Super 8. Once checked in, he agreed to leave me to get some rest. About thirty minutes after he left me at the door to my room, I did just what I had intended. I checked out of the Super 8. I went for a long drive before returning to my hotel just in case he was following me. Somehow, discovering I was not there anymore, Kirk called me and asked why I left the Super 8. I came up with some story about staying with my girlfriend since I did not want to be alone, and I was still very much shaken. He seemed eased by that and let me go with the agreement I would call him first thing in the morning.

The following morning, I decided to head straight for my credit union to empty my saving account and move it to a new one. Even though Kirk did not have access to that account, something just did not sit right with the other account. I then went to First Bank to ask about my card and try to withdraw a little more cash. After all, it was all my unemployment. Kirk did not work. I found out that my card was not taken by mistake; it was reported stolen by my "husband;" he had asked the card to be seized upon attempted use and had also drained all of the money from the account except for $33.76, which the teller thought was a strange dollar amount to leave. I instantly knew it was a slap in my face. I was 33 at the time and born in 1976. I took the money, removed my name from the account (since I could not close a joint account without him), and went on my way.

At the time, I felt a significance in the dollar amount and what I thought was a simple slap, was in fact a larger statement in the game of spiritual warfare. Think of the Passion Story, beloved, the Easter story of Christ's last week on this earth as a man. Throughout His teachings, Christ was questioned, ridiculed, and mocked. This last week of human life was the worst: He triumphantly entered Jerusalem on the back of a donkey colt as was foretold in the Old Testament, but He encountered the worst week of His human life. He was stressed to the point of sweating blood in the Garden of Gethsemane, He was arrested, beaten beyond human recognition, and hung to die on a cross. Our Lord was estimated to be 33 years old at the time of His earthly death. I was currently in my story, 33 years old. Though Christ knew the burden He would bear, I did not and still He used it to teach me.

When I got to the office I decided to call and get the incident number from the civil assistant, just so I had it for my records. It was my intention to file for a restraining order that week. When I called the police department, all seemed normal. I gave them my name and told them I wanted a copy of the incident report from the previous day. The desk sergeant said the officers had not really filed one; they usually do not when both parties agree on scene. All the officers do is log the call. I asked if I could file a report, so that I could protect both sides of the fence, meaning me and Kirk. In giving my information to the desk sergeant on the phone all was well, then upon giving her Kirk's, she stopped and interrupted me, saying I needed to speak with a detective. I, of course, asked why. Nothing had happened; it was a simple report. She replied that this detective handled all incidents regarding registered sex offenders.

I shouted, *"What?!?!?!"* The desk sergeant calmly replied, "I am sorry, ma'am, you will have to speak with him." I then was put on the phone with a detective with the sex crimes division. Explaining to him that I did not understand what was going on and why I was speaking to him, he patiently and carefully explained that I had been in a relationship with a violent sex offender who had brutally raped a woman in California. This must have been the woman he told me about that night in my old apartment. As the detective continued to speak, I became incredibly physically ill. He informed me Kirk was also out on bond from a theft charge he was facing with his previous wife. When I mentioned the bank incident and my card being falsely reported stolen, he gave me the number of the detective in charge of the investigation into the ongoing theft case.

Taking a moment to regain my composure and settle my stomach. I called her, and we spoke for quite a while. She asked me for bank statements and the like, assuring she was going to see about having new charges brought against him. She also asked me not to say anything to him and to stay away from him if possible. Explaining to her that I still had possessions in my house and a brand-new puppy I was concerned for, I promised to be careful and cautious.

Kirk still texted and called me almost all day, every day, throughout the week, using the puppy as an excuse to talk to me and see me. Saturday before Easter, April 3rd of 2010, trying one last time to get possession of the puppy, I spent the day with Kirk and the puppy. All the while, I was secretly checking in with a few friends on the burner phone I had previously purchased, one of whom worked for a local County Sheriff's department. It was set to silent in the bottom of my purse. We went for lunch and then a drive up Highway 66 into Estes Park. The road was icy, and he was not paying attention—intentionally, it seemed. At some points of the drive, I wondered if I would make it back to Aurora alive, or if he would intentionally drive us off a cliff. At the end of the day, I had agreed to meet him at church for Easter services the next morning and then he was to leave the house in the afternoon so that I could collect some more of my things and the puppy. He had gotten me a storage unit to "show faith" that he wanted me to feel secure and allowed—for the first time in our entire relationship—my name to be the only one on the account. Maybe I could get out unscathed any further.

The Serpent Strikes

Easter Sunday, April 4th, 2010, was a beautiful, sunny day. I texted Kirk and said that I was sick and going to stay in bed. I was in fact quite nauseous, having spent the previous day with a vile disgusting person that made my very skin crawl. He texted back saying that he missed me and hoped I felt better by the afternoon so that I could still come and get the puppy and my stuff. I went and took a shower and got ready for a visit that was a long time coming.

Christopher and I have been best friends for many years, and I was at one point close to his mom and brothers as well. This relationship with Kirk had ended these few relationships and I was hoping to make amends with his mom that Easter. I went by the store and got an Easter card and a stuffed lamb, and headed for Christopher's mom's house. Fully expecting the door to either not be answered or shut in my face, I knocked. I had caused his family a lot of pain when I just cut them all off without explanation. I would not have blamed her at all if she had reacted either way. Instead, in a mother's most understanding and loving way, she opened the door and, with a look of shock, she threw her arms around me and said I was the last person she ever thought she would see again. Crying, I told her I needed to apologize for my actions, and I told her that I had left him. We sat and talked all day and went for ice cream. That was our thing, caramel moo-lattes, and Oreo blizzards at Dairy Queen. I left around two-thirty and headed back towards Aurora. I texted Kirk and asked if I could still come by the house. He responded yes and told me that he would leave, a few minutes before my estimated arrival.

I pulled up to the house at about three or three-thirty and it looked as if he was not there. Checking in with a girlfriend, I proceeded to enter the house. It was quiet and shut up for the day; he appeared to be gone. I went in through the garage, wanting to get done with things as quickly as I could. In coming up from the garage into the kitchen, Kirk was there, standing against a counter. I gasped, surprised and scared, hoping he did not notice my expression. He quickly said, "I just want to help you. You aren't feeling well and some of these boxes are heavy, and I want to haul some in the van too, so you can get more stuff." I reluctantly agreed. I did not want to upset him. After all, I was not sure what he would do.

We went into the crawl space to get my totes and boxes. He helped me lift two of them up into the bedroom and took them out to his van. All the while, he kept his distance, not really talking to me. I know now his intent was to lull me into a more relaxed state by not pressuring me to talk. Back down into the crawl space we went for more. I mentioned that there was a box missing, a box of my dad's personal belongings. Kirk said that he thought he moved it to the far corner off to the left. Telling him I did not see anything over there, he insisted it had to be and suggested I walk over there and actually look closer. I did. No box.

Once I got over to the corner and hunched over, my back to him, Kirk came up behind me. He told me he missed me, he loved me, and he wanted to sleep with me. I rolled my eyes, not facing him of course, and told him I still did not feel that good and could we do that later in the bedroom or something. He pulled me around by my belt loop to face him and said, "I don't think you understand. I want to sleep with you *now.*" He held up a filet knife and told me to undress. I thought instantly about my family, and asked God to be with me and get me out of there alive. My family could not lose me like this, Robyn and Christopher could not lose me like this. I started to cry a little and asked why he was doing this. He told me to shut up and stop crying. I did. Once my shoes and jeans were off, he told me to lie back slowly so I did not bump my head. He had me touch him and get him hard and then he proceeded to rape me while holding the filet knife's blade about an inch from my lower left rib cage. His right arm and hand were shaking as he held the knife toward me. At one point I did feel the steel of the blade on my skin. It scratched but did not cut. When he was done, he told me to hurry up and get dressed. I did. Beloved, understand that sometimes the best thing to do to survive is submit to your attacker and not fight back physically. In your surviving, your fight and victory come afterwards, in a far more powerful way.

We came out of the crawl space and into the bedroom just above. He stood in the doorway, blocking my exit for what felt like an eternity. He kept asking, "What are we going to do? I just committed a felony." Numb and in complete shock, I asked God to manipulate my tongue to say whatever I needed to in order to get out. Out of my mouth like melted butter ran the words, "Do about what, baby? Nothing happened but sex between a happy couple. No one has to know. This is our business." He kept insisting that I was going to tell, and he could not have that. Only operating with the power of God, I moved closer to him, asking him to put the knife down, he was scaring me. I insisted I was not going to tell anyone. Finally, he did and grabbed a mag light flashlight instead. Still insisting he had committed a felony and wanted to know what we would do about it, I got right up next to him and stroked his shirt and his chest and just kept repeating, "No, baby, I love you. Nothing happened; we can work through this. It's okay, I am alright. I love you. Please, I am just shaken up. I need to get some fresh air." He asked if I would wash up before I left. If I agreed, he would let me go. I said of course I would, and that I would do anything to help him feel okay about what had just gone on.

He let me through the doorway and told me to go upstairs and wash up. I told him I would, and as steady as I could I walked up the stairs to the main bathroom and closed and locked the door behind me. Remembering everything my dad had always said in survival classes he taught about not cleaning up after being raped, I grabbed a wash rag and turned the water on. I wet the rag even put some soap in the sink and splashed the water around a bit. I then wrung out the washcloth and hung it on the sink and dried my hands on my jeans. I came out of the bathroom and down the stairs to the main level. Kirk was standing in the kitchen again. He asked if I would write a note of my side of the story in case we ever argued, and this came out.

I told him that if it made him feel better, I would be happy to write one. Grabbing a blank sheet of paper out of our Weekend To Remember conference notebook, I wrote a note stating that, on that date, we had consensual sex as a truly happy couple and I signed it. Kirk agreed at that time to let me go. He told me to grab the puppy and get my keys, and we could leave. After all, he still had to help me to the storage unit.

He called me the second we got to our vehicles and kept me on the phone to the storage unit. Once there, he helped me unload the totes and watched me as I locked it all up. He walked me back to my car and hugged me. As we parted ways, he called my cell and kept me on the phone until I finally convinced him I was safe and calmed down. I wanted to get the puppy inside where I was staying. He agreed to let me go after I promised I would call him in about twenty or thirty minutes after I got the puppy inside and settled and took a shower. Once off the phone I walked straight into the hotel office and asked the desk clerk to call 911 for me.

In shock and numb from the entire afternoon, I was very emotionless when the police, EMS, and fire department showed up. One of the firemen took my puppy upstairs to my room for me and set him up in the bathroom, while another asked why I had called from the office. All I remember saying was not trusting myself to be that close to shower and clean clothes without taking advantage of them. The officer that took the report was, in a word, awesome. He was patient, steady, and very compassionate. Still in "survival/cop's daughter" mode, I would have been fine if he were cold and very "just the facts, ma'am." How difficult it must be to come into a situation like that and be a male cop when very possibly the last person this woman wants to see is a man. This officer was very detail-orientated and very good at communication. He, of course, followed the ambulance to the hospital so that I could give a statement and have a rape kit done.

Beloved one, this is a necessary, yet humiliating experience to go through. I was blessed with the nurses and staff that walked me through this process. They were discrete, as gentle as possible, and explained every step of the process to me and what it was for. Upon taking his initial report, the officer mentioned above came in and explained everything to me. They were going to go to the house and knock and see if Kirk would talk to them, but they could not go in and get him until a warrant was issued. Kirk had every right to slam the door in their faces. Joking, I asked, "I can't just give you my key?" The officer cocked his head for a second, told me to hang on. He would be right back.

A few minutes later, he came back in and said that he was told as long as I am within twenty-five yards of the house, they could actually take my keys and use my permission as resident to go in. He asked if I was sure I could handle that. I told him whatever needs to be done, let's do it. In the meantime, I had called the detective I had been in contact with earlier in the week and let her know what was going on. The victim's advocate volunteer had pushed until she finally talked me into calling my parents and asking them to come to the hospital, against my actual comfort level. I am not that close with my mother. I love her; she is my mom. We have for sure had our issues, and I just knew that somehow, at some point, this would wind up my fault in her opinion, so I really did not want them called until I was ready to call them. Too tired to continue arguing my point and not in the mood to take a cab from the hospital, I reluctantly agreed.

Once released from the ER, my parents and I followed the officer I had been working with and his team to my block and parked at the corner. They walked up to the door and knocked. No one answered, so I gave the Sergeant my keys and they entered. Kirk was, of course, nowhere to be found, and neither was the washrag, knife, or note that I had written. The officer I had been working with came out with his Sergeant to tell me, and asked if I felt up to walking them through the afternoon's events. If not, it was okay, but I would have to do it as soon as I was up for it. I was there and it was fresh and I was still numb from shock, so I felt I might as well get it over with. In the same patient and compassionate manner he had all evening, this specific officer took point and walked me all through the house, allowing me to stop and breathe when I needed to. Finally done around twelve-thirty in the morning, I was able to go back to the hotel I was staying in to shower, change, and sleep.

After I took the longest, hottest shower of my life, I came out of the bathroom, got into my sweatpants and a hoodie, picked up my puppy, and sat on the bed. Laying back against the pillows, I felt as if I was at peace, a quiet calm, a shalom in my soul, as if I were being held. I slept soundly and dreamlessly that night, and got up to go to work the next day. When I came in, I informed my boss what had happened, and she asked why I was even there. Having just started, and knowing I was far better off there working and busy than I was at home dwelling on the assault, she understood, and let me continue in my day. The beauty of the company I worked for is that they are a family-owned, family-oriented company full of believers. I felt safe there.

> [1]*And seeing the multitudes, He went up on a mountain, and when He was seated His disciples came to Him.* [2]*Then He opened His mouth and taught them, saying:* [3]*"Blessed are the poor in spirit, for theirs is the kingdom of heaven.* [4]*Blessed are those who mourn, for they shall be comforted."*
>
> —*Matthew 5:1–4, NKJV*

A Demon Caged

The next sixty days were horrifying. Kirk was on the run and stalking me from a distance. The investigators and I just did not know what that distance was. One minute he seemed to know my every move, and the next he would say something in a text or a voicemail to make us think he was far away. That first week after the assault, my stepdad escorted me everywhere I went, following me in his car. Not really knowing where else to turn, I reached out to my church and they put me in touch with one of the pastors. He suggested I attend Celebrate Recovery that coming Friday night. I had always thought this was a group like AA for recovering addicts when, in fact, it is for all of us dealing with life and the issues it entails. I attended that Friday and connected with a woman who just gave off a vibe of safety and understanding.

The following Saturday evening, April 10th, I went shopping with my parents at a local WalMart. As we were walking through the store, I thought I had heard my name being paged to the dressing rooms. I thought to myself, "No it couldn't be." We walked over there perplexed, and admittedly a bit scared. When I approached the gal working the counter there, I asked her what name she had just paged and why. She had told me it was Deborah Hust, and it was at the request of a very sweet polite man on the phone who was trying to reach his wife. How did he know I was there unless he followed us? I immediately called the detective that has been working with me since that very first call I made to the Police Department two weeks prior. She told me to go to customer service and not to leave the store under any circumstances. She was calling the local police and would be right there. I waited with my parents in customer service while the PD searched the store, talked to the manager, watched the videos that covered the interior and exterior of the store, and waited for the detective. No sign of Kirk ever having been there.

That night, I went into a form of protective custody. The detective took me back to the hotel and helped me pack so that she could move me to another location. My car was driven by another officer to a secured location until further notice. At that moment, my world changed from just watching over my shoulder to back entrances of buildings and very little freedom. I was picked up every morning and driven to work. I had to have lunches delivered into the office or have someone go get them for me. The same routine for the evenings: picked up and driven back to the hotel. I could not go to church, eat out, go shopping. I felt like the prisoner. I understood why they did what they did for me, and I was—and still am—extremely grateful for it, but it was very frustrating at the time. I am a fighter and felt like I was not doing anything to get better or fight this monster. It was not until later down this path did I realize that fighting was exactly what I was doing. I was fighting to stay focused and alive to take Kirk down and hold him accountable.

> *[1]Hear my cry, O God; attend to my prayer. [2]From the end of the earth I will cry to You, when my heart is overwhelmed; lead me to the rock that is higher than I. [3]For You have been a shelter for me, a strong tower from the enemy. [4]I will abide in Your tabernacle forever; I will trust in the shelter of Your wings.*
>
> —*Psalm 61:1–5, NKJV*

One evening on the way back to the hotel I asked the detective escorting me, just how bad Kirk really is. At this time, the case was still open, the response given was that someday when the case was closed and he was in custody we would sit and chat, but right now I just could not be told. That answered all I needed to know at that moment: that answer meant Kirk was far worse than I could have ever thought. That bothered me even more; I figured that with all the attention I was getting it had to be bad. Little did I realize at the time the spiritual and physical warfare I was in the midst of.

While in protective custody, they swept my car for GPS tracking devices and one was found under the back seat of my car. It was purchased in Ft. Collins about a week before I was raped. This made sense in the timeline I was trying to piece together for myself, because the Friday before Palm Sunday, Kirk had thrown a temper tantrum and taken my car out for several hours and he would not return my phone calls or respond to text messages.

In late April, I was asked to speak to my employer and leave the state for a while. The investigators were stretched thin, and they needed me "out of the way" for the moment. I was offered witness protection and my parents wanted me to take it. They wanted me so safe and far away that they wanted me to accept, essentially, giving up my life. My parents and I had a huge fight about them trying to have me declared incompetent and forced into witness protection. What they just did not get was that Kirk had tried to take my life, why would I give it to him? It was bad enough I was hiding from life. The worst that could happen was he would get to me and send me home to be with Jesus. God had already proven to me my time was not up yet and I refused to let Kirk run me into a life of fear. I spoke with the main detective and agreed that I would leave to a place of my choosing for a "vacation" so that they could regroup and focus on pinning him down. I was allowed to "vacation" at my best friend Robyn's house in California. I mean, where safer to hide than a military cop's house on a military base, right? Her husband was active duty and stationed there at the time. My local law enforcement team worked with the base law enforcement team to ensure everyone was on the same page.

Beloved, I want to take a moment right here and tell you that I have stood solid since the day of my rape in the fact that April 4th is just a date, but Easter Sunday is Resurrection Day. Resurrection Day is the day the Lord Jesus rose from the dead for me and for you. The enemy will not take that day from me. I refused to give up fighting because Jesus did not give up on me. He submitted to the will of the Father. Though He asked God to take this task from Him, and when it was not, He submitted and allowed the soldiers to arrest him in the Garden at Gethsemane.

> [39]*He went a little farther and fell on His face, and prayed, saying, "O My Father, if it is possible, let this cup pass from Me; nevertheless, not as I will, but as You will."*
>
> *Matthew 26:39, NKJV*

While I was away on "vacation," the investigators already involved stepped it up a notch and enlisted the help of the U.S. Marshalls Fugitive Task Force. There was even talk about the possibility of placing the story on the television show *America's Most Wanted*. They wanted Kirk and they wanted him badly. When I came home, I was updated on the status. Kirk was still at large. I was able to have my car back, but still had to be in a hotel of the detective's choosing and was still technically in protective custody, having specific times to call and check in and specific places to be at designated times. I was allowed this little freedom only because they had confirmation he was out of the state of Colorado, at least at that point. I was able to meet one of the detectives from the Local Fugitive Task Force face to face for coffee. He had assured me they would get him, thanked me for all my cooperation. The last thing he said as we parted ways was, "Hey Deb, we're closer than you think; take that and rest."

This way of life became normal throughout the month of May. I could finally move into my own apartment, and the investigators and the County had a security system installed that had some special features added, like two passwords. One to deactivate a false alarm, and one to signal that our fugitive friend was there with me. I took the state-required class to apply for a concealed-carry license. I grew up with firearms and was in the Marine Corps, so a sidearm made sense to me. It is a whole new experience to go shopping for a new purse and have to make sure you can conceal your weapon in it. Not a solution I would recommend to all survivors, because an angry assailant coming at you can make that deadly weapon your worst enemy if you hesitate for even a second. I would warn away from a firearm without sufficient training and tons of practice because you definitely do not want to become a gunshot victim from your own weapon being turned on you.

Friday June 4th, 2010 I was coming back from picking up lunch. I had just sat my purse and my food on my desk when I saw the Fugitive Task Force Detective's number come up on my desk Caller ID. Not really in the mood for bad news I answered the phone, "Hey Detective, what's up?"

"Hey Deb, you sitting down?"

"No, what's up?"

"Sit down."

"Okay."

"We got him!"

"*What?!?!?!*"

"We got him!"

"Sweet Jesus, oh Lord, thank You!!!" I continued screaming, "How? When? Was anyone hurt?"

"Without incident, in Portland about fifteen minutes ago. Remember when I told you we were close? Well, we *were* close. Now go have a great weekend and we will update you further on Monday."

By this time with all the shouting, practically the whole office had congregated around my cubicle and were eyeing me with anticipation. Shaking and crying, I smiled and shared the news: Kirk was in custody and no one was injured in the process. We all hugged, and my beloved boss sent me home. Very obviously I was going to be useless the rest of the day. I had my life back; I had phone calls to make and news to share!

That Sunday, I went back to my home church after weeks of being told to stay away. I felt so refreshed and free again. I decided to go home after service, grab my puppy, go for a drive somewhere in the foothills, and maybe hike a bit, but God had other plans for me that day. I had not been able to cry since the day I was assaulted, and even then, it was not much. I needed a good, deep, cleansing cry. I had not felt safe enough to let my guard down and cry. Instead of driving to the mountains, as intended, I ended up at Ft. Logan National Cemetery. It is where my mother's parents are buried. I went to the headstone of my grandfather the "Colonel," and saluted, kissed it as I always do, then walked to the other side where my grandmother's name is and placed my hand on the word "Janet." I fell to my knees and started sobbing uncontrollably. It was like my head was in her lap again and I was being consoled by my gramma, her hands stroking my hair and telling me it was all going to be okay, just remember that above all else Jesus loves me and so does she.

The Lord knew I needed a safe place to just let go. He led me to a cemetery where no one in their right mind would give a second thought to a woman, with a puppy, kneeling by a headstone and crying. He led me to one of the sources of my strength and comfort, my grandmother. I did not know it at the time, but that moment would lead me on a path in discovering just how instrumental both my grandmothers were, and how much I am like them both in strength, personality, and compassion.

Kirk was extradited back to Colorado in mid-June. We then started the long judicial process. Sitting in the first attempt of a preliminary hearing, it hit me, as my stomach was turning at the very thought of being in the same building with him again: this is not about me anymore. This is about stopping a sociopathic rapist and domestic abuser. This is about stopping the enemy in his tracks. I sat and prayed to God right there in the witness room to have the strength and fortitude it would take. As long as there was a breath in my body, Kirk would never walk the streets truly free again. The fighter awoke again in my soul and I became determined that no matter what, no matter how long, and no matter how many delays and tricks he tried to play, I would see this through until the end. I was alive for a reason and, quite possibly, part of that reason was putting him away and protecting any future women that may cross his path.

¹Then David spoke to the Lord the words of this song, on the day when the Lord had delivered him from the hand of all his enemies, and from the hand of Saul. ²And he said: "The Lord is my rock and my fortress and my deliverer; ³the God of my strength, in whom I will trust; my shield and the horn of my salvation, my stronghold and my refuge; my Savior, you save me from violence. ⁴I will call upon the Lord, who is worthy to be praised; so shall I be saved from my enemies." ⁵When the waves of death surrounded me, the floods of ungodliness made me afraid. ⁶The sorrows of Sheol surrounded me; the snares of death confronted me. ⁷In my distress I called upon the Lord, and cried out to my God; He heard my voice from His temple, and my cry entered His ears. ⁸Then the earth shook and trembled; the foundations of heaven quaked and were shaken, because He was angry. ⁹Smoke went up from His nostrils, and devouring fire from His mouth; coals were kindled by it.

—2 Samuel 22:1–9, NKJV

The Battle Rages

My story has definitely been a refining fire from above. The Lord has been so faithful and good to me throughout this, I could never *ever* again doubt Him. Question His plan, maybe—we are all human and that is bound to happen—but never again could I ever doubt that He is in control.

As I originally wrote this section, we were headed into the 21st month of the battle within the judicial system. In our beloved country, there are such things as victim's rights, defendant's rights, innocent until proven guilty, and due process in prosecution. Once the accused are caught, or surrender, they are given a bond hearing and possible arraignment (very rarely is the arraignment done separate from the bond hearing) in which the charges against them are read, they are given a bond amount, if applicable, and the opportunity to ask the judge for defense council to be appointed if one has not yet been obtained. The accused will also be given the opportunity to enter a plea of guilty or not guilty at this stage. If the accused pleads guilty, the rest of the game is quite simple: plea agreements are discussed, and the judge will either accept the terms and impose sentencing or set the sentencing for another date to allow for plea agreements to be discussed. If the accused pleads *not* guilty, then the "games" begin. The next step is a preliminary hearing in order to determine if there is enough evidence to warrant going to trial, a pretrial conference to allow the accused to waive their right to a speedy trial and to ensure they understand what is going on and what they are facing, a pretrial motions hearing, sometimes two, to decide what evidence and testimony is or is not allowed at trial, and then—finally—a trial.

If the accused does not waive right to speedy trial, they are to be tried within six months; if they do, the process can drag out for several years. Kirk was initially assigned one public defender; they requested and were granted several postponements for various reasons: the defense council had not read the discovery yet, another time was they needed the DNA results from the rape kit, another was a scheduling conflict. Finally, after three attempts, we had a preliminary hearing.

Then set for pretrial conference, that hearing went off without a hitch and, wouldn't you know it, Kirk waived his right to speedy trial. Set for the first pretrial motions hearing, a DA investigator was able to go back over my statement and several other factors, and note that they were able to charge Kirk with two additional felonies—finally, a cookie for our side. Well, with this cookie comes his right to *two* defense attorneys: due to the severity of the charges, he rates *two* public defenders to ensure he is protected! Frustrating, very. I remember being so angry at the fact that I cannot take a lawyer in to protect me even if I could afford one, and here, he gets two, at taxpayers' expense. At *my* expense! This simply meant more delays, the first postponement requested this time was because only one of the defense attorneys could make it to court, the second delay was due to the fact the newer of the two had not had an opportunity to read the discovery yet. The last delay was bittersweet. The DA was quite sick so they could not proceed, but this time the judge was quite appreciative of my patience and willingness to be flexible in all the delays and even stated this has gone on long enough and that this next date, we would be going to trial.

At each hearing, I have had a little "birdie" or two in the courtroom, as I had not had to be there at all. I was initially kept in an anteroom (waiting room) for the preliminary hearings as I may have had to testify. By the grace of God I did not, so I had not seen Kirk since the date of the rape. My little birdies kept me informed as to what goes on in the court room: what the judge said, the DA, defense council, etc. Since Kirk was in custody, he had to be brought over from the jail for each hearing, while I did not have to attend and had been advised, by council and two very dear friends, that it would be best for me to stay away until the time comes when I must testify at trial. Small relief that I would, for the moment, have a break from the ups and downs.

Amid the battle, the Lord stood faithful always. I had at one point been gifted the opportunity to go to my very first Women of Faith Conference in September of 2010. At this point, things seemed to be at a standstill. I felt stuck in a void and numb again. I needed something to show me life again. I had prayed for something, a little sign of something good. I felt like a child asking her dad for a cookie from the cookie jar for a skinned knee or something. God is a good, good Father. World Vision is an amazing organization that helps partner children with sponsors worldwide. They encourage communication between sponsors and their children. The first night at Women of Faith, a precious set of big brown eyes was on a packet in my seat. I thought, "Oh, she is cute, but I could never. I do not have time and money to be a sponsor. . ." I placed her packet to the side, in the empty seat next to me. Late that night when I got home, I found that same set of eyes in my purse. I thought it odd: how did she get in there? I made mental note to get her back to the World Vision table first thing in the morning, so she could get a sponsor.

That night, I could not sleep. Her big brown eyes just kept weighing on my heart. It was like God saying, "Daughter, you asked Me for a cookie, a comfort, some joy. Take her, love her; she is My gift to you in this war." Her name is Jelin, she lives in Guatemala. I call her "Mi preciosa galleta de Dios"— My precious little cookie from God. Beloved, let me tell you that being her sponsor blessed me in so many ways through this journey. I got to watch her grow up in pictures and read letters of her joy and educational growth. In January of 2021, in my year of renewal, a bittersweet communication came. It was a final letter from my little blessing. It was a farewell letter; her community is now self-sustaining, thanks to prayer and all the sponsors through World Vision. While I was sad at no more letters, I am overjoyed at their success. I do have two other beautiful baby girls now and continuously enjoy their communications, though none will ever be "mi preciosa galleta de Dios."

This battle waged on for almost two years. Up and down emotionally and in and out of court. I used to have a recurring dream I remember to this day, in vivid color and clear speech. I would dream that I walked into the courtroom and walked right up to the defendant's table, my Bible open to the book of Revelation, and slamming it into Kirk's face saying, "When you studied your enemy to try and defeat him, you must have skipped this part, because you lose!" Then I would smile and walk away. Beloved, in this writing journey, I have found that God allowed that dream to come true for me—in a sense. In preparation for writing, I had ordered the transcripts from the sentencing hearing, as that day was a blur to me. I did not know what Kirk had said, if he in fact did speak, and I did not remember much of what happened other than he was put away in a cell. The day before they arrived in my email, I was out walking at lunch and, out of nowhere, the chapter and verse from my dream came to the forefront of my mind. I didn't know the significance of it hitting me right then, but when the transcripts arrived the next day, I skimmed the fifty-seven pages and found it. Allow me to explain.

In October of 2012, Kirk finally pled guilty to multiple counts against him in exchange for some other counts being dismissed. Instead of a lengthy trial and possible life, he was sentenced to 18 years in the Colorado Department of Corrections. He wanted to "spare me" from the "pain and anguish of a trial." Ha ha. What a joke. I was allowed to speak to the judge at sentencing, and in doing so, I was able to speak out loud the words in Revelation that I had dreamt about so many times.

> *¹Then I saw an angel coming down from heaven, having the key to the bottomless pit and a great chain in his hand. ²He laid hold of the dragon, that serpent of old, who is the Devil and Satan, and bound him for a thousand years; ³and he cast him into the bottomless pit, and shut him up, and set a seal on him, so that he should deceive the nations no more till the thousand years were finished. But after these things he must be released for a little while.*
> —*Revelation 20:1–3, NKJV*

Our words have power, more so than many people realize. Sure, you can read a page or write something down and it has impact, but to breathe life to it and speak it out expresses power. Giving life to the words in the book of life gave me such a sense of peace, knowing the enemy is bound and put in a vault. I was also able to go on and mention that, further into the book of Revelation, it speaks of the enemy's ultimate defeat and demise as God's reign continues and that all are judged according to their works and evildoers are cast into the lake of fire for eternity. In my moment of speaking outwardly to the judge and the people in the court room, I was able to breathe life into the words that seal the enemy's fate. Speak them over him and remind him: God wins; the enemy does not.

> *⁷Now when the thousand years have expired, Satan will be released from his prison ⁸and will go out to deceive the nations which are in the four corners of the earth, Gog and Magog, to gather them together to battle, whose number is as the sand of the sea. ⁹They went up on the breadth of the earth and surrounded the camp of the saints and the beloved city. And fire came down from God out of heaven and devoured them. ¹⁰The devil, who deceived them, was cast into the lake of fire and brimstone where the beast and the false prophet are. And they will be tormented day and night forever and ever. ¹¹Then I saw a great white throne and Him who sat on it, from whose face the earth and the heaven fled away. And there was found no place for them. ¹²And I saw the dead, small and great, standing*

before God, and books were opened. And another book was opened, which is the Book of Life. And the dead were judged according to their works, by the things which were written in the books. [13] The sea gave up the dead who were in it, and Death and Hades delivered up the dead who were in them. And they were judged, each one according to his works. [14] Then Death and Hades were cast into the lake of fire. This is the second death. [15] And anyone not found written in the Book of Life was cast into the lake of fire.
—Revelation 20:7–15, NKJV

This was not the only gift of power I was given that day; I was given three. The second was that I was able to exercise the right to leave the courtroom when and if Kirk chose to speak. Of course, he did, so before he started, I got up, hand in hand with a couple of friends and boldly walked out to the hallway. I could not imagine what foulness would seep from his mouth, and I wanted no part of it. I was hoping that he would see defeat and just sit back down. As I found in reading the transcripts he, of course, did *not* sit back down. Nevertheless, the judge allowed him his time and then made him wait for her final ruling, so that I could be brought back into the courtroom. The look of shock and disbelief on his face when she also reviled him and stated what she felt needed to happen versus what the law states was beautiful justice all by itself.

The third gift of power I received that day was the knowledge that I truly had forgiven this individual, and feeling the freedom that it gave me. I have been tested in this forgiveness. Before sentencing, I was asked from several different directions what I wanted done with this individual. All I had to do is say a word and he would have been ended. Instead, I chose to say, "I want nothing done; it's God's job, not ours, to inflict punishment. He will get his just deserts in God's way and time." That was a hard pill to swallow for these individuals that had known me as a second daughter and little sister. Yet they respected and honored me in my request to leave Kirk alone. I had a peace, knowing that in the power of forgiveness, I was heaping hot coals down the backside of my enemy. My forgiveness and surrender to God was far more punishment for Kirk than anything man could do. It meant he lost all power over me. It was like what that pastor I quoted had said:

"Forgiveness is not forgetting;
it's appealing to a higher court."

Now if you will note, I started this chapter mentioning that both the defendant and victim have rights. I also mentioned a list of things that have been done to allow Kirk to execute his rights with very little mention of mine. Unfortunately, the way the system works, while victims do have many rights, it does not always feel that way. Honestly, I have not felt that mine have been even thought of, let alone honored. Before every hearing, I am asked by the DA how I would feel if the case were to be continued, and the answer is always the same: "I want this over with; I don't want it continued." To which the reply comes, "Okay, I will let the judge know." He does and, until this last hearing, I felt as though the words seemed to fall into the air and not be heard at all.

Beloved, know that the DAs and the judges do their very best to make decisions based on fact and, while I felt completely ignored, I knew that I was not. The system must allow the games to be played so that the defense can execute all the defendant's rights and dot every "i" and cross every "t" so that when it is all said and done, he or she will not have a leg to stand on for an appeal. Most of the victim's rights come into play prior to prosecution and after sentencing.

The Criminal Defendant's Basic Rights
As defined by the 6th Amendment of the Constitution:

- The right to a speedy and public trial.
- The right to a lawyer.
- One is to be provided by the courts if defendant unable to afford one.
- The right to impartial jury.
- The right to know who your accusers are,
- . . .and to face them in court.
- The right to know the nature of the charges.

The Victim's Basic Rights
As defined by COVA
(Colorado Organization of Victim Assistance)
{other states may vary slightly}

- To be notified of and present at court proceedings in your case.
- To consult with the Prosecution about the disposition of the case.
- To be heard at the defendant's sentencing, modification of sentence, acceptance of a plea, bond reduction or modification, or parole hearing.

- Have the court determine restitution.
- Upon written request, be informed of the status of the case, post sentencing (ColoradoCrimeVictims.org).
- Information about what steps can be taken in case there is any intimidation or harassment.
- Information about and referrals to services and assistance.
- The right to be informed about the legal remedies available.

As I write these words, it has been just under nine years since Kirk was sentenced and moved from County Jail to State Prison. In this time, I have faced him again in three parole hearings and have written letters twice to Community Corrections. I will face him again and again, at every parole hearing and every Community Corrections board, until they must release him. My fight remains the same. To keep him from harming anyone else, ever! I know that they will eventually have to release him on what is called a mandatory release date. At that point he will be put into a special parole plan called Sex Offender Intense Supervised Parole (SOISP). He will be monitored in society 24/7, via the latest and greatest ankle-monitoring GPS system.

God is in control and justice will, and does always, eventually come through. Whether in man's courts or God's, justice will always be served by the Father.

> [20]*And the God of peace will crush Satan under your feet shortly.*
> *The grace of our Lord Jesus Christ be with you. Amen.*
> —*Romans 16:20, NKJV*

Since the date of the assault, I have stood firm in the fact that April 4th may be the day, but Easter will never belong to the enemy. That is *my* day. Easter has never again fallen on April 4th until this year, 2021—this year of closure and redemption. This year I walk through this book with you and dig up the little stuff that has waited in the wings to be dealt with. I have made lists. I have unpacked research done long ago on Kirk's criminal history. I have prayed over it. I have asked for release. This year I walked through Easter Sunday, April 4th in Divine Victory. I had pockets of the day in which memories or flashbacks appeared, and tears ran. But they did not run in pain and anguish; they ran in a healing, cleansing manner. My tears flowed from my eyes like brisk, clean waterfalls from mountaintops where snow was melting to spring, washing my pain and cleansing my soul. My tears on Easter 2021 were of healing rain in my heart.

The following weekend, I went to the home of a dear friend, a soul sister, for lunch with my family. The sole purpose was to be surrounded by laughter and mighty prayer warriors as I burned to ashes the paper products from this journey. All the court documents, my research, my lists, the CDs of recorded calls from Kirk. I had even burned the transcripts from the sentencing I just received. What a cleansing experience to see the fire completely sever all soul ties! It was God's consuming fire burning away the old and preparing for new growth.

> *³ Therefore understand today that the Lord your God is He who goes over before you as a consuming fire. He will destroy them and bring them down before you; so, you shall drive them out and destroy them quickly, as the Lord has said to you.*
>
> —*Deuteronomy 9:3, NKJV*

God, Show Me,
No Matter What. . .

The enemy is quite the chameleon when he seeks to destroy. I went through the illness and death of my father, the split from family, the betrayal of dear friends, none of which worked to sway me from turning and saying, "Alright, well, we made it through that one, God, can we have some peace now?", only for the devil himself to show up in the form of comfort and support: Kirk. The subtleness and swiftness of his control over me happened *so* incredibly fast—looking back now, I sometimes wonder how did I not see that coming.

The days immediately following the assault, I was understandably in shock. It felt surreal, as if I were in a dream. Time seemed to stand still. I did return to work the next day. After all, I had just started a new job and was not about to lose it. I felt safe there with those people. I could occupy my mind on "real" things and "real" people. I went into my boss's office after she had come in that day, to tell her what was going on. She asked what I was doing, and I explained to her that I was the kind of person that just could not sit around and wallow. Understanding, she said if I ever needed to just go, all I needed to do was say so and I could have the time. In the evenings, I would go back to the hotel where I was staying, cuddle with my puppy, try to watch TV or read and pray. It was hard to focus.

About a week or so after the assault, I finally just plainly cried out and asked God, "I know You were there, but I need to see where You were. I cannot make sense of this and I need to see You. Where *were* You? I need to know!" Then I just sat and cried myself to sleep. In my dreams that night,

He answered me and started showing me right where He was. He was in the thick of it all.

During the rape, Kirk had a filet knife in his hand which he held less than two inches from my lower left rib cage the entire time we were in the crawl space. I even felt the steel at one point, but it only scratched; it did not cut. God revealed to me He was right there. Kirk's hand trembled with what I initially thought was an adrenalin rush of power and control, but what God showed me was that his arm shook in resistance. God held his elbow back from making deep contact with my skin the entire assault. Then it was God that helped me stand and walk to the door, and it was God that spoke for me when Kirk held me in the room just outside the crawlspace. He also revealed to me that He was with me in the bathroom when Kirk made me go "clean up." God was the silent voice within that told me, "Don't you dare wash away any evidence. I will get you home and I will get you safely out. Trust Me; fake your way through this. The wash rags are in the closet where you left them, baby girl, wet one and turn the sink on and let it run a few minutes. Splash it a bit with your left hand." (I hadn't touched anything with that hand, so it was safe to wet it.)

He showed me that after returning from the hospital and finally getting to shower, the peace and restful sleep I had was because I was resting on His chest, wrapped in His arms, and I was able to sleep a peaceful and dreamless sleep. He held me like a Father holds his newborn baby: wrapped in peace, unconditional love, and safety.

I had in the initial days thanked God for my dad and the Marine Corps for the training I had had most of my life, but I did not think to thank God for that still, small voice within. I woke the next morning in tears. I knew it: I knew He had been there the whole time, I knew He would not have let me go through that alone. I have since asked continuously for Him to show me more of where He was. Then the question becomes, "Why, *why*, Lord, did I have to go through this?"

Almost immediately, I started looking for answers. I insisted on counseling, but it had to be faith-based. I prayed with girlfriends and even attended a Celebrate Recovery group at my church. My first night at Celebrate Recovery was the Friday right after the assault and it was the only time I was allowed to return to my home church during the entire 60 days Kirk was on the run. I met a woman there that night who became quite instrumental in some of the healing that I have done and some of the fun in life I had found again. Something told her to reach out and give me her number and hug me, so she did. The very next night was when I was officially put in protective custody and could only have a few phone numbers of people I was allowed to tell anything to, and hers was, for some reason, the first one I grabbed. She helped me learn to trust again. She prayed with me on the phone and was always available for a word of encouragement and support. She had walked in similar shoes and could respond to me like a trusted girlfriend that gets it and understands. She would listen to my cries, my screams, and my anger without judgment. She just enfolded me in love and understanding.

As I mentioned previously, at one point I was shipped out of state so that the investigators could focus on him and not so much on me. Understandable, for sure, but what about my job? The detectives came into a meeting with my employers and me. All of us agreed that the safety, both of my fellow employees and me, was the priority. The owner of the company hugged me and told me it was not my fault. He said that my job would be waiting for me and that he and his family would pray for my speedy and safe return. Part of me had felt like I was letting Kirk win: I was angry that he was "taking" part of my life from me. I do *not* run away. I stand and fight. I felt like I was running.

When I was safely away, my best friend Robyn and my newfound friend helped me through conversation, prayer, and refocusing my attention to current daily life. They helped me see that I was not running, I was standing and fighting: I was doing what was necessary to locate and catch my assailant. I needed this time away to refocus and the authorities involved needed me refocused because the hard part had not even started yet. Once he was caught, we would start the long judiciary process that would put a long-time danger away from the public for what we hoped would be the rest of his natural-born life.

The enemy has placed stumbling blocks within my path. I have had such severe night terrors that I wake in a cold sweat and panic so bad I cannot breathe. I have doubted myself in things I know I am capable of doing. Daily, it was a struggle to even get up in the morning and deal with the tasks of life in general. Many times, my best friend would remind me by email and text message of a cute little thing we had found for each other in times of trial and tribulation:

"Girlfriend, live your life in such a way that when your feet hit the floor in the morning, satan shudders and says, 'Oh, crap, she's up. . .'"

And so I did: I got up every day, and I did struggle (still do, sometimes) with daunting menial tasks of everyday living. Walking the dog was an adventure, can of mace in my pocket, firing at the ready of my right index finger, calling a friend just before walking out the door and calling back just as soon as we were back inside again. I prayed and read my devotions all the while, not realizing the work God was doing in my heart.

If you recall from an earlier chapter, I also mentioned that the Lord gave me the word "romance" to describe this walk. In all things, He is great and sees the beauty in all things. Sitting at a restaurant, eating a meal alone, I asked God to give me a word to start this book my Pastor suggested. If it was truly God's intention that I write my story, I needed Him to give me the word to center around. Instantly, "romance" came to my mind. Along with the word was a beautiful picture of a romantic ballroom-dancing couple.

You are probably thinking, as I did, "Romance? Really? Okay, explain this one to me, because I definitely don't see romance anywhere." A week later, He did exactly that. In beautiful pictures, God showed me from the very first man I saw after the attack, He has placed compassionate, patient men in my path to "romance" me away from hate. I realized in that moment, while I have been stark raving angry beyond description, I have yet to hate Kirk. Still, to this day, I harbor no hate for his human person. I hate what he has done to so many, and the damage he has left in his wake, absolutely. But I have not hated *him.*

The Lord placed the initial responding officer, the lead detective, the owner of my place of employment at the time, men in the church I attended, my best friend Christopher, and the husbands of a few trusted friends in my path to show me that not all men are of that nature. There are so many stories, beloved, of women who harbor hate and contempt towards men in general because of repetitive abuse and assaults of various kinds on their person. I cannot say that their feelings are wrong—I am not them—but what I can say is that hate is destructive and does damage to the hater, not the hated. These men were patient, protective, compassionate, all when they did not really have to be, just so that God could use them through their personalities to romance me completely away from hate.

Beloved, righteous anger is justified, and anger is a stage within the grieving process. The Lord Jesus Himself got angry and did damage in the temple:

> *¹²Then Jesus went into the temple of God and drove out all those who bought and sold in the temple and overturned the tables of the money changers and the seats of those who sold doves. ¹³And He said to them, "It is written, 'My house shall be called a house of prayer,' but you have made it a 'den of thieves.'"*
> —*Matthew 21:12–13, NKJV*

As time continues, God has and continues to show me where exactly He was in each part of my story. I will share more of that beauty in a later chapter. Beloved, all you need to do is ask Him, and when He sees you are ready to handle it, in His timing, He will show you. I have asked and had immediate answers, but sometimes I ask and wait what seems like an eternity for the answer. Yet along with the delays comes a peace, and understanding is also given: sometimes I was not ready when I asked, so He gave me the answer when He knew I was.

"No matter what. . ." Three simple words that have so much power when you least realize it. People say them all the time, almost as commonly as "I love you." Honestly, I never paid much attention to them throughout my life. My dad would say he loved me "no matter what" I did wrong; my mom, same thing. Friends would say we would always be friends "no matter what" life brings us. It was not until Kirk that I realized the power in these words.

Kirk would have the sweetest things to say and always follow it up with a "no matter what." Throughout our entire relationship, he would throw those words out in almost every conversation we would have. After the assault, while on the run, he would call my work phone (he did not have my new cell number) and leave voicemails, saying things like:

"Remember we will always be together, no matter what!"

"You can't hide from me forever, I'll always come for you no matter what!"

"I love you, always, no matter what!"

I grew to hate these words; they disgusted me. They would make me cringe in fear or my stomach turn in absolute sickness. I asked everyone I knew to please stop using them around me. I even remember shaking and screaming at my best friend's husband one time in their kitchen because he said those words to their daughter after they had an extremely loving conversation.

If you will recall, a big part of what I told you we would get would be God's redemption, and this is a big piece of it. These three words haunted me for thirteen long months. Every time I heard them spoken, I heard his voice saying them, and they made me ill. Then one day on the way to yet another attempt at a court hearing, my angel friend M driving, a song came on: *No Matter What* by Miss Kerrie Roberts (KerrieRoberts.com).

I had turned the volume up because of the way the song started. When the chorus came, I felt like my heart stopped for a moment. I started to shake and sob hysterically. I cranked the volume up more; M just smiled and squeezed my leg as she drove on. It is a song about tribulation and how what the singer was going through had completely caught her off guard, but she knows God has filtered it through His hands so she will trust Him and love Him. . . *no matter what. . .*

> *⁴And God will wipe away every tear from their eyes; there shall be no more death, nor sorrow, nor crying. There shall be no more pain, for the former things have passed away. ⁵Then He who sat on the throne said, "Behold, I make all things new." And He said to me, "Write, for these words are true and faithful." ⁶And He said to me, "It is done! I am the Alpha and the Omega, the Beginning, and the End. I will give of the fountain of the water of life freely to him who thirsts. ⁷He who overcomes shall inherit all things, and I will be his God and he shall be My son."*
> —Revelation 21:4–7, NKJV

God has more than redeemed those three words; He has made it my battle cry, my *fight song*. Through the words of this song, He has ministered to me in so many ways. I have felt inspired and empowered. I have felt protected and loved. I have felt so much emotion in the power that those three words give me now. I use these words with power and might as I try my best to fiercely love my family and my friends, no matter what.

God's amazing redemption of all things and healing through many facets can bring you comfort and peace, and at the same time, empower the warrior within. A few years after finding my battle song, I was again in a place of frustration and was at my best friend's house when I heard another most perfect melody: *Warrior* by Miss Hannah Kerr (HannahKerrMusic.com/videos).

Again, beloved: a song of empowerment to tell you He loves you. This beautiful woman mentions standing in the face of fear and getting stronger each time she falls, using His power and might to strengthen her in her weakness. The armor of God is all you need amid the battle, beloved. The Lord goes before you and is always your rear guard.

> [10] *Finally, my brethren, be strong in the Lord and in the power of His might.* [11] *Put on the whole armor of God, that you may be able to stand against the wiles of the devil.* [12] *For we do not wrestle against flesh and blood, but against principalities, against powers, against the rulers of the darkness of this age, against spiritual hosts of wickedness in the heavenly places.* [13] *Therefore take up the whole armor of God, that you may be able to withstand in the evil day, and having done all, to stand.* [14] *Stand therefore, having girded your waist with truth, having put on the breastplate of righteousness,* [15] *and having shod your feet with the preparation of the gospel of peace;* [16] *above all, taking the shield of faith with which, you will be able to quench all the fiery darts of the wicked one.* [17] *And take the helmet of salvation, and the sword of the Spirit, which is the word of God;* [18] *praying always with all prayer and supplication in the Spirit, being watchful to this end with all perseverance and supplication for all the saints.*
>
> —*Ephesians 6:10–18, NKJV*

NOTHING CAN PIERCE YOUR ARMOR WHEN YOU HAVE BEEN DRESSED FOR BATTLE BY THE HOLY SPIRIT

Cynda Hunter

Forgiveness is for *Us*

In March of 2011, it happened out of the blue. I forgave Kirk and submitted all my anger to God. It happened during a semester of Bible study. We were studying the significant women in Christ's genealogy: Tamar, Rahab, Ruth and Naomi, Bathsheba, and Mary. The story of Naomi and Ruth occurs during the time of the judges. The surviving women of Elimelech's family, after having deserted God's land during a famine, return to the land of Judah after the death of Elimelech and his sons. Naomi requests her daughters-in-law to stay in their homeland and remarry: one does, but not Ruth. She keeps her covenant made to the family and follows Naomi home. Naomi has Ruth present herself to Boaz for redemption in the family. Boaz and Ruth are married, and Ruth is then able to carry on the family name and becomes an ancestor of King David and Jesus.

During the large-group discussion that evening, our leader explained that the redemption of Ruth was not that far from our own, in which Christ redeemed us by dying on the cross for our sins. We are again restored within the family of God. She then made time for an alter call to pray for our own redemption in Christ, or to pray for the redemption of loved ones. This act was not a usual thing in our Bible studies. I mean, come on! We are *women!* We like the discussion and fellowshipping over snacks. I felt that ever-gentle tug at my heart to kneel and pray, so I came forward and knelt at the altar. I started to pray for some friends of mine and was stopped mid-sentence. I felt my heart tug grow stronger, and heard that small, gentle voice say, "Daughter, stop. That is not why I called you down here tonight and you know that. . . It is time—time to pray for the one who hurt you so. Pray for him and forgive him. It's My turn to carry this weight for you; surrender it to Me. . ."

83

I did not want to; I was not ready. I was still angry, and I still *wanted* to be angry. After a bit of resistance, I started sobbing and nodding my head. "Okay. I will." I prayed for the first time for Father God to take my anger and hurt, and then freely admitted my forgiveness of Kirk. I ended with a prayer for his redemption.

> [43] *"You have heard that it was said, 'You shall love your neighbor and hate your enemy.' [44] But I say to you, love your enemies, bless those who curse you, do good to those who hate you, and pray for those who spitefully use you and persecute you, [45] that you may be sons of your Father in heaven; for He makes His sun rise on the evil and on the good, and sends rain on the just and on the unjust. [46] For if you love those who love you, what reward have you? Do not even the tax collectors do the same? [47] And if you greet your brethren only, what do you do more than others? Do not even the tax collectors do so? [48] Therefore you shall be perfect, just as your Father in heaven is perfect."*
>
> *—Matthew 5:43–48, NKJV*

By the time I lifted my head, I had been surrounded by several other women and we were all holding each other.

> [20] *". . .for where two or three are gathered together in My name, I am there in the midst of them."*
>
> *—Matthew 18:20, NKJV*

The peace that comes with complete forgiveness is unexplainable. In the Greek language it is known as "siopao" (pronounced see-o-pah'-o). As I lay in bed that night, I was given a promise: God promised me that I would have redemption one day. He promised all the things taken from me in this battle would be restored. He spoke to me in that sweet, soft voice and promised me a Redeemer, a Boaz of my own someday. I slept so soundly and quietly that night, for the first time in almost a year.

I know God commands us to forgive our enemies and pray for them, and I knew that forgiveness is not for our enemy, it is for *me.* I deserve the peace that comes with that surrendered heart. Judgment and punishment are God's, not ours. Hatred and unforgiveness breeds a black, cold, unhealthy heart in us. As mentioned earlier: Forgiveness is not forgetting; it's appealing to a Higher court.

If you carry that knowledge in your heart, and trust God to carry you to that place when you are ready, He will. Beloved, He will hold you through it all and wipe your tears away when you finally release that deep sigh of relief. God knows that, as humans, we will not always forgive the very second we are hurt. He is patient and loving and will carry you through different steps of healing before bringing you to forgiveness. I knew eventually it would happen, but I surely did not see it happening in less than a year.

Shortly after I forgave Kirk, we went on a retreat. That was the best weekend ever, alone in the beautiful mountains of Colorado with a bunch of women I had grown to love as sisters, mothers, and friends. During the retreat, a few of us were asked to share our testimonies, and I was one of them. It was Sunday morning after breakfast and worship; I made it through sharing with the grace of God. When you do something that defies what satan wants you to do, you can be what is described as battle-fatigued. I was more so than I thought.

There was a cute little skit done by a couple of the ladies there, a depiction of the entire life of Christ as told by modern-day mimes. When they got to the crucifixion, a large kitchen knife came out of the box and was raised in the air in a malicious manner. It started the worst panic attack I had had to date. I could not catch my breath and could not get out of the room fast enough. My dear friend and mentor met me about halfway across the floor and rushed me out the door to pray with me while I just sobbed and sobbed. Hardly able to stand, leaning up against the wall, we stood in prayer for quite a while.

Later, when I finally got home, I emailed my EMDR (Eye Movement Desensitization Reprocessing) specialist. This needed to be dealt with. She had me come in a few days later and we worked on connecting the dots to this memory. What I had not realized is that in all the work I had done to this point, I had never dealt with the knife. I had two pictures bouncing around in my head: identical pictures of the knife, Kirk's shaking arm and my lower rib cage. One image was given by God to show His presence, and one left by satan to strike fear in me. They had to be tied together. I went through the hour-long session late on a Friday and tried to fit the pieces together there. EMDR therapy will send you through a whirlwind of emotions all at once. While very effective, it is very exhausting. I went home and slept for what felt like days.

Saturday, I felt the need to just be quiet and let God work in my mind to piece these pictures together. Sunday, the same: I got up and went to church and spent some time on my knees at the altar, still waiting. A few more days went by. I did the normal everyday "have to's:" get up, go to work, come home, etc. Wednesday, early in the morning, I was typing an email to my good friend and mentor, when it happened. God tied the pieces together for me. Mid-paragraph, I stopped and started sobbing uncontrollably. My hands were still moving, but I could not see what I was typing, nor could I stop. I did not try real hard though, either. When my hands finally stopped moving and I was able to grab a tissue, wipe my eyes, and look, there it was on the screen:

Christ took a spear to the lower rib cage, bled and died for me so that when I faced a 'spear' in mine, I didn't have to. . .

I nodded and started to weep, thanking God for His gift to us and His clarification of these two pictures.

> [32] *Then the soldiers came and broke the legs of the first and of the other who was crucified with Him.* [33] *But when they came to Jesus and saw that He was already dead, they did not break His legs.* [34] *But one of the soldiers pierced His side with a spear, and immediately blood and water came out.* [35] *And he who has seen has testified, and his testimony is true; and he knows that he is telling the truth, so that you may believe.* [36] *For these things were done that the Scripture should be fulfilled, "Not one of His bones shall be broken."* [37] *And again another Scripture says, "They shall look on Him whom they pierced."*
> —*John 19:32–37, NKJV*

I closed the email simply stating that I needed to go, and I would explain the random interruption later, but that praise was due to the Father.

As I write these pages now, we head into what is known by believers as Passion Week. This describes the week from Palm Sunday, when Jesus rode into Jerusalem on a donkey colt, through His arrest, beating, crucifixion on Friday and resurrection on Resurrection (Easter) Sunday. It has now been several years since the assault in 2011. The Lord pointed out to me, again, in my writing last night, that I was 33 when this happened, as Christ was 33 when he suffered and died for me during the Passion story.

Luke 19:28–Luke 24:12: "The Passion Story"

In reflection on this point, my husband and I were discussing it and God revealed to us that this journey has been a choice. Just as Christ was beaten and suffered and died for us, He chose obedience to the Father's will and this path because He loves us. As fully man, Jesus could have chosen to walk away from the Father's plan, in free will, yet because He was also fully love and God, He chose to follow the Father's will and direction, knowing it meant immense pain and ultimately a gruesome death. Beloved, He chose us. He chose you and He chose me, to bear our pain and burdens, allowing our suffering to be His and showing us blameless before the Father's throne. He rose, overcoming death: raised into new life, as a beautiful picture of the Father's undying love and faithfulness for all His children. Just as I have chosen to rise up and not allow the enemy to destroy me. Using Christ's example in the Passion story, to lead me in healing and walk towards the Father's most perfect love and faithfulness.

> *²⁸When He had said this, He went on ahead, going up to Jerusalem. ²⁹And it came to pass, when He drew near to Bethphage and Bethany, at the mountain called Olivet, that He sent two of His disciples, ³⁰saying, "Go into the village opposite you, whereas you enter you will find a colt tied, on which no one has ever sat. Loose it and bring it here. ³¹And if anyone asks you, 'Why are you loosing it?' thus you shall say to him, 'Because the Lord has need of it.'" ³²So those who were sent went their way and found it just as He had said to them. ³³But as they were loosing the colt, the owners of it said to them, "Why are you loosing the colt?" ³⁴And they said, "The Lord has need of him." ³⁵Then they brought him to Jesus. And they threw their own clothes on the colt, and they set Jesus on him. ³⁶And as He went, many spread their clothes on the road.*
> —Luke 19:28–36, NKJV

> *⁴¹And He was withdrawn from them about a stone's throw, and He knelt down and prayed, ⁴²saying, "Father, if it is Your will, take this cup away from Me; nevertheless, not My will, but Yours, be done." ⁴³Then an angel appeared to Him from heaven, strengthening Him. ⁴⁴And being in agony, He prayed more earnestly. Then His sweat became like great drops of blood falling down to the ground.*
> —Luke 21:41–44, NKJV

> *⁴⁴Now it was about the sixth hour, and there was darkness over all the earth until the ninth hour. ⁴⁵Then the sun was darkened, and*

the veil of the temple was torn in two. ⁴⁶And when Jesus had cried out with a loud voice, He said, "Father, 'into Your hands I commit My spirit.'" Having said this, He breathed His last.

—Luke 23:44–46, NKJV

¹Now on the first day of the week, very early in the morning, they, and certain other women with them, came to the tomb bringing the spices which they had prepared. ²But they found the stone rolled away from the tomb. ³Then they went in and did not find the body of the Lord Jesus. ⁴And it happened, as they were greatly perplexed about this, that behold, two men stood by them in shining garments. ⁵Then, as they were afraid and bowed their faces to the earth, they said to them, "Why do you seek the living among the dead? ⁶He is not here, but is risen! Remember how He spoke to you when He was still in Galilee, ⁷saying, 'The Son of Man must be delivered into the hands of sinful men, and be crucified, and the third day rise again.'"

—Luke 24:1–7, NKJV

Beloved, no matter what the devil uses against you for fear, trust the Lord God Almighty to turn it around and make beautiful lessons out of it. I have never looked at the crucifixion picture the same since that day in April 2011. There is a whole new significance to God's gift to us in Christ Jesus.

Kinsman Redeemer; My Boaz

In *His* time, as promised, it happened: redemption began. I had for several years been in a relationship with a decent man, who has a good heart, but I felt he was not engaging and basically was not involved in anything. After several lonely years and much prayer and guidance, I decided it was time to move on for both our sakes. We separated and, while co-residing, made plans to move on in our own directions.

Months later, Saturday, 22 February 2020, at an event raising awareness and money to help stop veterans' suicide, I met *him*. I met Robert. In the "Run for the 22" you run/bike/walk 22 miles and do 22 push-ups every mile, as we lose, on average, 22 veterans a day nationwide to suicide. There was only one treadmill and one stationary bike left, I let my girlfriend have the treadmill and I went to the bike. Sitting on the bike next to me was a gentleman, with a semi-long Fu Manchu, and a great smile, plugging away at his miles. We chatted, motivated each other throughout the counts and just had a good time. I could not place why this stranger made me feel so at ease. We each did extra miles and push-ups just to keep chatting. Then when I had finally had enough and my shoulder said I was done at 35 miles and approximately 400 push-ups, I said I needed to go. He asked if I would be at the after-event and I said, "Sure, I will come." Then I went to the floor in the other room, stretched out and left.

Later that afternoon, I met up with my girlfriend again and we went to the after-celebration event. There he was, decked out in his leathers and his cut (vest). He bought me a seltzer and then he seemed to disappear. As I went inside to hear the speaking, there he was, making a presentation about his own struggles as a combat vet. Still not understanding why, I felt at ease around him, and listened intently to his story. I saw some other friends, visited with them, and lost my girlfriend somewhere in the crowd, so I left. The next day, I woke up thinking about him. I reached out to the gal that headed up the event and asked if she had his contact information. I was in the process of planning some CrossFit events and thought he might be interested. I texted him on that Monday to ask him about possibly meeting to discuss these Cross-Fit ideas.

We flirted a bit and agreed to meet for dinner later that week. Working out at the gym that Tuesday night, I felt a presence come up behind me. Now, understand that since all this has happened to me, I do not like people coming up behind me, and I am not one it is good to surprise. As I was coming up out of the ab machine, about to lose it all over someone, I saw in the mirror it was him and I was weirdly at peace suddenly. This freaked me out more than someone coming up behind me. We sat and talked and when I asked him why he was there, he chuckled and told me it was technically his gym too and he thought we had dinner plans.

Our flirtatious courtship went on daily from there. Lots of little things he said and did were pieces from my past. I could not place this ease, this peace he gave me, and just his very presence was really starting to perplex me more and more. I do not pursue relationships: every true friend I have has always been a give-and-take type of relationship and my circle has remained quite small since Kirk. After a few short weeks, I even felt comfortable enough to share my brokenness and my story—*this* story. We met at a local truck stop and sat in his truck, watching the snow fall. He sat quietly and listened. He handed me tissues as I needed them, but never said a word until I was finished. He prayed with me and sat in silence for a bit, tears in his eyes at the thought another human could cause so much damage. He shared his brokenness with me. We sat for hours and talked each other through pain from the past.

Finally, after a few weeks, I asked God to explain to me this peace that I have with this man. As I slept, He reminded me of His promise to me the night I forgave Kirk at the altar during Bible study. He promised me that night that someday, He would send someone that would love my whole heart and redeem all that was distorted and taken from me. He showed me this face with the long Fu Manchu and the beautiful smile. He showed me that my Boaz had come in the form of this man with whom I felt so much peace.

> *9And Boaz said to the elders and all the people, "You are witnesses this day that I have bought all that was Elimelech's, and all that*

was Chilion's and Mahlon's, from the hand of Naomi. [10]Moreover, Ruth the Moabitess, the widow of Mahlon, I have acquired as my wife, to perpetuate the name of the dead through his inheritance, that the name of the dead may not be cut off from among his brethren and from his position at the gate. You are witnesses this day."

—*Ruth 4:9–10, NKJV*

Having met Robert at a veteran's event and having an unusual draw to him, it was much like how things started with Kirk. Even more parallels, between then and now, started to reveal themselves so that I could see the redemption in my story.

Just a Few of the Parallels: My Given Boaz: Robert

1. Rides a maroon and red Harley Davidson.
2. Adorns me with simple, yet beautiful jewelry.
3. Explores nutrition and fitness with me.
4. Is proud of his Marine and my service.
5. Lifts me up when I feel unpretty or judge myself.
6. Helps me pick out nail designs and hair color, ultimately leaving me to decide.
7. Always opens my door out of respect and drops me at building entrances to keep me from weather.
8. Hugs everyone, in a brotherly appropriate way.
9. Complements my natural beauty and encourages me to go with what makes me comfortable, makeup or not.
10. Is an expert with knives and various martial arts, wants to teach me for my own confidence and knowledge.
11. Reads with and to me, books, and articles we pick.
12. Loves to drink tea, and explores new kinds, introducing me to looseleaf teas, though I still prefer coffee.
13. Hand-washing dishes is soothing and relaxing.
14. Talks to me multiple times a day, just to communicate well.
15. Reads, studies, breaks out, and discusses Scripture with me daily.

The Enemy's Serpent: Kirk

1. Rode a maroon, red, and tan Harley Davidson.
2. Hated me wearing any jewelry, it was "too much."
3. Dictated what vitamins and foods I could take and eat.
4. Belittled my service, I was "too proud" of being a Marine.
5. Belittled and body-shamed me, especially if I felt unpretty.
6. If he did not choose the nail design or hairstyle, I was not allowed to do it.
7. Always opened my door out of control, and shamed me if I did not "allow" him to.
8. Hugged everyone, especially other women, close and tight.
9. Constantly insisted no makeup, I was "too pretty" or "cheap" if I wore it, and that it was not necessary.
10. Bragged about how good he was with knives and how much he learned as a surgical orderly.
11. Insisted on reading to me, never letting me choose readings.
12. Insisted on tea at night, only certain flavors and I was instructed on how to steep it a certain way.
13. Hand-washing dishes was the only approved way.
14. Insisted on constant contact, to monopolize my phone.
15. Twisted and perverted Scripture for control and abuse daily.

The beauty in the redemption of parallels, beloved, is that you can see the false next to the true, and you can see how one is tainted and stained in lies and darkness, and the other glorious in truth and light. I will not deny that, once revealed, it will freak you out a bit, but trust the Lord to walk you through the redemption process and He will also ease that anxiety surrounding the new things that remind you of the old.

The first time I saw Rob's maroon Harley (we call her "the Chariot"), my heart skipped a beat, and I was taken aback only for a moment to the first time I saw Kirk's. It has been little subtle moments like this, beloved, that the Lord has brought me to and allowed me to remember the old, yet feel peace in the new. This man, this amazing gift I now have in my life, has taken everything and flipped it, replaced it, and he continues to fix the cracks as they come up.

One of the most beautiful pieces of this "redemption pie" is Rob's road name, Preach. It is beautiful for so many reasons. He is an Ordained Minister and the Chaplain for one of our local chapters of the Combat Vets Motorcycle Association (CVMA). Rob has been the Associate Pastor of a church and the leader of Children's Ministry. He can walk into bike rallies and places a Pastor would not normally go and minister to the lost and the broken. From when I rode years ago on my cut (vest) I have a patch that says simply, "Prayer Warrior." It is still there. I am one that you can ask to pray for you. I will, without question or hesitation. The pairing of Preach and a Prayer Warrior could not be more perfect in the bike world.

Kirk was also a leader in the church he attended prior to our meeting. He was in the choir and led a men's motorcycle ministry. He was even able to unwittingly manipulate a Pastor from the church we attended. This Pastor spoke on Kirk's behalf at sentencing and had been so far twisted into Kirk's web, he had stated *I* was at fault for a good portion of what was happening. The devil will counterfeit anything the Lord has created in a simple ploy to try and defeat what God has planned.

Beloved, when the Lord says to you that He will renew and restore, *He does!* My life has never been this surreal. I have been beaten down, battered, and abused, both emotionally and physically. These actions were not only caused by Kirk, but also by friends and family. Rob has come to restore me from my pain and scars and lift me up where God wants me to be. I am supported. I am encouraged. I am loved beyond measure. My strength comes from the Lord only and always, yet He has given me Rob to restore and rebuild my physical and emotional wounds here on earth. Please understand: we are both still quite human and we do disagree at times. Yet, through our faith and God's love, we can talk anything through. We laugh through tears and lift each other up past our wounds.

The Lord has gifted me a warrior in this man. One who stands, kneels, and fights for the Kingdom. Rob prays with me and over me daily. The power and comfort I feel when we are joined in prayer is indescribable. Our hearts and souls have been truly intertwined by the Father. I now understand what my grandmothers meant when they spoke of physical pain they experienced whenever my grandfathers were away from them for extended periods of time. Rob is retired from over thirty years of federal service and travels to motorcycle rallies and other sorts of missions work he is called to do. Though he is never too far and not gone for long, it still makes me ache physically to be without him. It is the worst at night and in the morning, when I wake. He, in turn, experiences the same feelings.

There is a peace in my soul knowing that I have a partner, not just a friend and a spouse. We truly are each other's helpmates. We can each listen to the tone of the other's voice and tell when a hug and a word of encouragement is needed. I can give a look and he will stop anything he is doing to hold me and allow me the opportunity to exhale and relax. I want what he wants, and he wants what I want. We both love our children and grandchildren, together as one big family. We both have experienced horrific wounds and had decided life was better walking alone; we figured there was far more peace and happiness in that. Then the Lord intervened.

Rob not only supports me in the community work I do, but he has also gotten involved in it. He has extended the reach into the organizations he is associated with, making a bigger impact for the community. He loves to stand in the back and watch as the beautiful chaos unfolds, and we all serve our community families together. We enjoy the same recreational activities and each respect the other when space and time alone are needed. We always come together in the evenings and share, caring genuinely for each other's needs.

> [9] *Two are better than one, because they have a good reward for their labor.* [10] *For if they fall, one will lift up his companion. But woe to him who is alone when he falls, for he has no one to help him up.* [11] *Again, if two lie down together, they will keep warm; but how can one be warm alone?* [12] *Though one may be overpowered by another, two can withstand him. And a threefold cord is not quickly broken.*
>
> —*Ecclesiastes 4:9–12, NKJV*

In December of 2020, God started speaking to Rob, Christopher, and Robyn individually. He was telling them that 2021 would be the year to stand fast in strength for me. It was to be a year of completion and victory. In January 2021, the Lord started to tell me the same thing. That was my year to complete the little things, finish this book for you, and walk on in victory. When I mentioned this individually to the three of them, all three smiled and nodded in agreement. I am not sure what that means exactly, as the Lord has only revealed a little at a time. In His gentle way of allowing all the pieces to be dealt with. Nevertheless 2021 was a year of completion and finality for this season in my story.

Our Father, Abba, Heals

¹⁵For you did not receive the spirit of bondage again to fear, but you received the Spirit of adoption by whom we cry out, "Abba, Father." ¹⁶The Spirit Himself bears witness with our spirit that we are children of God, ¹⁷and if children, then heirs—heirs of God and joint heirs with Christ, if indeed we suffer with Him, that we may also be glorified together. ¹⁸For I consider that the sufferings of this present time are not worthy to be compared with the glory which shall be revealed in us.

—Romans 8:15–18, NKJV

In *His* time, as promised, my beloved, the Lord our Father, our Daddy, our King can and will heal you of all traumas in your life. God wants nothing more from you than a relationship, a simple Father/child relationship. The Hebrew word "Abba" means simply "Daddy." A daddy who loves unconditionally and wholeheartedly. Laying His life down for the safety of and wellness of His children. Father God wants simply for you to reach out, like a child, and cry out to Him in your fear, your anger, your sadness, your pain. He will come and hold you so tightly and love you like no other has ever shown.

This can and will be scary for most, and that's okay. Many in this world have not had decent or healthy relationships with their earthly fathers, perhaps because of unhealed traumas in their own pasts, not allowing them to love the way they were intended to as fathers, and leaders of their families. I was blessed in that, not only was my birth father a great daddy, but also my step-dad. Both men showed my brother and me true unconditional love. They were not always easy on us, but never once did we have to doubt they would be there if we needed them.

On the night of my assault, all I wanted was my daddy, my safe place, my Superman, and my protector. Since his passing had been less than a year before that night, these pains were renewed very deeply in that moment. I cried and screamed for my daddy to come hold me and make it all okay. He did: Abba Father, our God, came and loved me through that moment in my tears and my pain. He held me tight all night long, just like my earthly daddy had done when I had nightmares as a child. He loved me in that dark painful place, and He just sat quiet and let me sob uncontrollably, until I had cried myself to sleep. If you'll recall, I mentioned earlier that I had one of the most peaceful night's sleeps ever in my life, the night I was attacked. I was able in that moment, in that night, to cry out in pain and rest against the chest of the One who created love. I was able to lean into, press into what I had been given in my heart as a little girl, I was able to rest in the arms of our Father, our Abba.

> [18]*I will be a Father to you, and you shall be My sons and daughters, says the Lord Almighty.*
> —*2 Corinthians 6:18, NKJV*

I will admit this process is not easy at all and is not rainbows and lollipops. It's not supposed to be. God wants us to dig in and dig out the muck and the mire and the deep yuck that we have suffered and give it to Him. There is a book and a movie out there that are an incredible and perfect example of this exact process: *The Shack* by William P. Young.

In this story, the main character experiences trauma as a child and then a horrific loss as an adult. The character is brought to a shack in which an encounter with Papa takes place. Papa is the name used for God by one of the other main characters, as that relationship is strong and comfortable. Papa appears to this main character as a safe person from the past, someone who always offered peace and comfort in bouts of turmoil. At the shack is also the Holy Spirit and the Son, in human form as comfort and peace. Through this experience, the character learns to trust and understand it's all about how much Papa loves and wants to have a relationship with His children, even in all the mess. Throughout the meat of the story, the individual is put face to face with the different traumas and Papa is right there the entire time, to comfort, reassure, and hold His beloved child. That is all He wants to do for all of us: to walk us safely and lovingly through any traumas we have encountered in life.

The enemy, satan, wants you to hang on to the pain and the hurt, deceiving you along the way, hoping that you would allow that pain and anger to destroy you and all the beauty that you were created for. The enemy is a thief and a liar; his mission is to keep you from healing, and have you walk in dark despair and unforgiveness. He wants to take away the joy that God has blessed us all with, by walking in fear, pain, and anger, and thus allow the enemy his playground.

> [10] *The thief does not come except to steal, and to kill, and to destroy. I have come that they may have life, and that they may have it more abundantly.*
>
> —*John 10:10, NKJV*

Earlier on, I talked about how forgiving your offenders or oppressors is for you, not them. This is necessary knowledge to conquer your traumas and allow God to move within them; this is a necessary process in healing. Forgiving is not forgetting and pretending trauma didn't happen. Forgiving simply means that you choose to allow God to take that trauma and the pain it holds and change it into a beautiful driving force for you to stand strong in Him. Forgiveness is a freeing of the spirit, heart, and mind; it is truly releasing the negativity surrounding your trauma to allow God to move and refine you, as if you were in a blacksmith's forge. The heat from the fire is not comfortable at all: it softens, blackens, and turns the metal into a moldable form. Removing it from the fire allows the blacksmith to mold, shape and beautify the metal as it cools and then, dousing it quickly with cool water completes his artistry. Be it a tool, weapon, or something to display beautifully on a wall somewhere, the blacksmith must first allow the metal to be heated in the fire. Standing watch, caring for his craft, he then removes and perfects the piece. God does this for us, beloved.

As in my story, God will not stop the free will of man, but He can and will watch, protect, and carry you through the fire of trauma. He stood with me in my fire, He held the knife back from completely piercing my side. God spoke for me and got me out of the room I was held in directly after the assault. God was in every single moment of my assault, and has walked with me or carried me in my healing. In my forgiving Kirk, it in no way means I have forgotten for a second what he has done to me and countless other women. It simply means that now instead of anger and fear, I walk in a peace that allows me to push forward and stand up for other survivors of violent crime and seek counsel for and with them. My remembering what he has done allows me the ability to utilize my frustration to fight against his release and to stand up and tell my story through tears so that others are aware of the danger lying in wait within that individual.

Healing is possible, though it is not easy, and it is not comfortable. God is big enough to handle the screams and shaking fists in your anger and hurt. You can be angry, and you can scream, yell and cry like a child in a temper tantrum. God can handle it all. Jesus got angry. Jesus wept. Jesus asked in the end as He hung on the cross, "My God, My God, why have You forsaken Me?" It is okay to question the why, it is okay to feel and walk in those feelings as you process towards healing. The key is not to do additional harm to the situation by sinning in your anger. Let Him love on you through it all. Healing is a beautiful gift from our Father and with trust in Him, He will fulfill the promise of abundant beautiful and purposeful life. No matter what!

> [3]And I heard a loud voice from heaven saying, "Behold, the tabernacle of God is with men, and He will dwell with them, and they shall be His people. God Himself will be with them and be their God. [4]And God will wipe away every tear from their eyes; there shall be no more death, nor sorrow, nor crying. There shall be no more pain, for the former things have passed away."
> —Revelation 21:3–4, NKJV

Footprints in the Sand
by Margaret Fishback Powers
(the last two stanzas)

"Lord, you said once I decided to follow You, You'd walk with me all the way. But I noticed that during the saddest and most troublesome times of my life, there was only one set of footprints. I don't understand why, when I needed You the most, You would leave me."

He whispered, "My precious child, I love you and will never leave you, never, ever, during your trials and testings. When you saw only one set of footprints, it was then that I carried you."

I Leave You with This. . .

Though this season may come to an end, my story will continue—as will yours, my beloved sister, brother, and friend. This is not an easy walk and nor is it anything our Father ever intended in the lives of His most precious children. Whether you grew up in faith, have never given it a second thought, or have for some reason allowed an experience to lead you away from His arms, please consider looking to Him. Life will not always make sense and you will encounter many different views and opinions on how you should handle different things. Know and trust in this: there is a book, as relevant today as the day it was written. The Holy Bible!

There is not a single question you can ask that cannot be answered by the words in Scripture. It comes in many different languages and versions. My personal favorites are both the King James and the New King James translations, though the Word is always the same and Scripture is never altered. The truth is laid out for us in black and white.

Remember, healing comes in pieces and stages, and you must first give yourself the grace to take your feelings as they come. Do not ever let anyone push you and say you are not healing fast enough, or you are not doing it right. Healing is a journey between you and God alone. No one can put a time limit on what you need or how God will work; it is in His time, beloved. God will walk you through it all and He will lead you to victory through His most perfect love. No one is you, no one's story is the same as anyone else's, you heal in your time, knowing that God is right there with you, no matter what. Lean into Him, press hard into Him. He will hold you, sustain you, fight for you, and love you in such an indescribable manner.

This was spoken over me many years ago as I was dealing with the news of my Daddy's illness and coming to realize he was not invincible. I struggled a lot with my faith in that time. My dad was my Superman, but I always knew in the back of my mind I would have to say goodbye someday—I just never imagined it would be so soon. This scripture never left my heart. I believe it is the very voice spoken to me in those dark moments of Kirk's terror that allowed me to find my focus and get safely to this point. I share it today with you in hopes that it will speak to the value you have been created with.

> [9]*But you are a chosen generation, a royal priesthood, a holy nation, His own special people, that you may proclaim the praises of Him who called you out of darkness into His marvelous light;* [10]*who once were not a people but are now the people of God, who had not obtained mercy but now have obtained mercy.*
> —*1 Peter 2:9–10, NKJV*

Beloved, if for whatever reason you have ever doubted your worth, please reread this passage as many times as it takes to know that *you* are chosen for a purpose and a plan. The Lord God Almighty created you perfect in His eyes. As a child of God, you are royal, for He is the King of Kings and your Father, no matter what the world may drag you through or drop at your feet. God can and will always, love, heal, redeem, and create a testimony to His Glory in your story. You are *His!* His Prince, His Princess. His child. *His Beloved!*

God the Father loves you best!

I thank you for your love and time. I am praying for each one of you who picks up and reads these words, that you would have revelation and healing in your own stories. Remember, our Father God will hold you and comfort you through anything. All you must do is stretch out your hand, cry out His name, and be willing to sit and let Him heal and love you. He does, like no one else ever could.

> [22]*And the Lord spoke to Moses, saying:* [23]*"Speak to Aaron and his sons, saying, 'This is the way you shall bless the children of Israel. Say to them:* [24]*"The Lord bless you and keep you;* [25]*The Lord make His face shine upon you, and be gracious to you;* [26]*The Lord lift up His countenance upon you, and give you peace." '* [27]*So they shall put My name on the children of Israel, and I will bless them."*
> —*Numbers 6:22–27, NKJV*

I love you! Be blessed, always!

His Warrior in Love,
Deborah
דבורה

Yes, I am a Princess, My Father is the King of Kings and the Lord of Lords

Resources and Information

If you or someone you know has been assaulted, please reach out! Local to you, experienced help is just a phone call or click away:

National Sexual Assault Confidential Hotline: RAINN
1-800-656-HOPE (4673)
www.RAINN.org

If you or someone you know is a survivor of violent crime in the State of Colorado, again please reach out! Local help is just a phone call or a click away:

COVA
Colorado Organization of Victim Assistance
www.ColoradoCrimeVictims.org
303-861-1160 or 1-800-261-2682

Outside the State of Colorado, please reach out to your local resources via any search engine! Look for keywords "Victim's Services" or "Crime Victims Resources".

One of my dear friends and soul sisters, Victoria, has a mission of her own helping to empower and strengthen survivors. As one with an incredible story herself, she has been led to reach out through her given talents and provide awesome opportunities for all of us! She also runs a healing room of sorts: **Ebb and Flow Healing.**

My Empower Tees is an online clothing and apparel shop that designs empowering and uplifting symbols to spread encouragement, strength, and love in the world. When you wear an Empower Tee you spread the message that survivors are not alone. In addition, every sale, all year long, will always be donated to Alternatives to Violence in Loveland, CO to help them in their mission to protect victims of domestic violence and sexual assault.

Join us in Supporting Survivors One T-Shirt at a Time:
www.MyEmpowerTees.com.

At Ebb and Flow Healing I provide life coaching and energy healing to clients that are ready to reclaim their power, access their inner strength to heal, and move forward and thrive in life. Healing from past trauma and deep false beliefs will not always be easy but it does not have to be alone. I will walk beside you on your personal healing journey and celebrate with you as we rise from the ashes together! Learn more or schedule a complimentary clarity session at:

www.EAndFHealing.com

The Lord's Prayer
(Matthew 6:9–13, NKJV)

⁹In this manner, therefore, pray: Our Father in heaven, Hallowed be Your name. ¹⁰Your kingdom come. Your will be done On earth as it is in heaven. ¹¹Give us this day our daily bread. ¹²And forgive us our debts, As we forgive our debtors. ¹³And do not lead us into temptation, But deliver us from the evil one. For Yours is the kingdom and the power and the glory forever. Amen.

SOME DAYS SHE
IS WEARY AND WOUNDED
AND WORN FROM
THE BATTLE.
EVEN STILL SHE REFUSES
TO RETREAT
BECAUSE CHRIST
NEVER RETREATS ON HER.

Seeds Among the Soil

Psalm 23, NKJV

¹The Lord is my shepherd; I shall not want. ²He makes me to lie down in green pastures; He leads me beside the still waters. ³He restores my soul; He leads me in the paths of righteousness for His name's sake. ⁴Yea, though I walk through the valley of the shadow of death, I will fear no evil; for You are with me; Your rod and Your staff, they comfort me. ⁵You prepare a table before me in the presence of my enemies; You anoint my head with oil; my cup runs over. ⁶Surely goodness and mercy shall follow me all the days of my life; and I will dwell in the house of the Lord forever.

EMDR Explained

Eye Movement Desensitization and Reprocessing (EMDR) therapy is an interactive psychotherapy technique used to relieve psychological stress. It is an effective treatment for trauma and Post-Traumatic Stress Disorder (PTSD).

During EMDR therapy sessions, you relive traumatic or triggering experiences in brief doses while the therapist directs your eye movements. This is not hypnosis; at no time do you leave your conscious self. EMDR is thought to be effective because recalling distressing events is often less emotionally upsetting when your attention is diverted. This allows you to be exposed to the memories or thoughts without having a strong psychological response. Over time, this technique is believed to lessen the impact that the memories or thoughts have on you.

EMDR was described to me personally by one of my treatment specialists like this:

> Trauma essentially forces our brain to disconnect from itself chemically, in a way. You have your inner brain that houses everything and then the outer brain that houses all your "compartments:" cognitive thinking, short/long-term memory, etc. When you hit a "trigger," that chemical separation causes the inner brain to "misfire," sending a cognitive thought out of short-term memory or something like that. What EMDR does is it causes a bilateral stimulation, forcing the brain to settle back on itself and redirect the memory correctly, store it, and save it appropriately. At the end of the day, it is God's job to heal you, the Holy Spirit's job to stitch your mind back together and my job to hand you the needle and the thread.

I, personally, can relate the relief from EMDR therapy as a "runner's high." A lot of people do not realize that a runner's high is a real thing. Most avid runners live with very few stress reactions and can calm their minds with a long steady run. I have found, in talking to another couple of therapist friends, that is because the bilateral force caused by running affects the chemicals in your brain the way the bilateral stimulation of eye movement does, causing your brain to settle on itself and relieve stressors. My favorite thing to do now to relieve any level of stress in my life is to put my earbuds in, crank the worship music, and go for at least a good 4-to-6-mile run. I love running outdoors on a long, dirt country road.

Please know, beloved, I am not telling you here to pick up running or any other sport. What I simply want to do is give life examples of what this specific therapy is like. It is freeing, but only when administered by trained professionals, because it is also very hard and forces you to deal with all the issues.

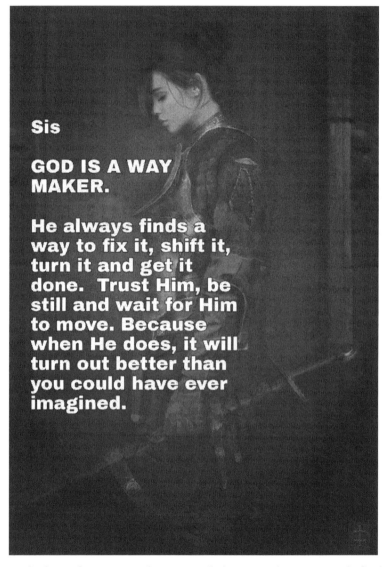

Sis

GOD IS A WAY MAKER.

He always finds a way to fix it, shift it, turn it and get it done. Trust Him, be still and wait for Him to move. Because when He does, it will turn out better than you could have ever imagined.

With this information I have provided, I pray that you reach for help when and where you need it, for that is not the sign of weakness the world would have you think it is, but instead a sign of strength and a sign of wisdom and the warrior spirit we were all born with. You are worth all the process to heal. You are a gift to the world and the Lord our Father delights in your smile and your heart. He wants you to heal from all your pains. He will walk you through it all. You will rejoice again, you will feel joy, peace, and hope.

> [1]*When the Lord brought back the captivity of Zion, we were like those who dream.* [2]*Then our mouth was filled with laughter, and our tongue with singing. Then they said among the nations, "The Lord has done great things for them."* [3]*The Lord has done great things for us, and we are glad.* [4]*Bring back our captivity, O Lord, as the streams in the South.* [5]*Those who sow in tears shall reap in joy.* [6]*He who continually goes forth weeping, bearing seed for sowing, shall doubtless come again with rejoicing, bringing his sheaves with him.*
>
> *—Psalm 126:1–6, NKJV*

Made in the USA
Middletown, DE
19 January 2023

22456681R10071